Putting the the pedal

CW00862571

Cycling Route 66 with Love Hope and Strength

by

Lydia Franklin

ISBN: 978-1-291-70811-0

Copyright © 2013 Lydia Franklin

All rights reserved, including the right to reproduce this book, or portions thereof in any form. No part of this text may be reproduced, transmitted, downloaded, decompiled, reverse engineered, or stored, in any form or introduced into any information storage and retrieval system, in any form or by any means, whether electronic or mechanical without the express written permission of the author.

PublishNation. London
www.publishnation.co.uk

Love *(n)*   *1. A strong feeling of affection*

2. A great interest and pleasure in something

Hope *(n)*   *A feeling of expectation and desire*

Strength *(n)*   *1. The quality or state of being physically strong*

2. The capacity of an object to withstand great force

Foreword

Lydia Franklin is a breed apart.

A woman so dedicated to life that her personality, and the experiences she becomes involved in, are imbibed with same qualities that define her as an extraordinary human being.

This book is not only a travelogue of Route 66 and America, but an unforgettable adventure tale that defies belief.

As an account of human endeavour it is phenomenal. As an insight into the depths one must draw upon to see a challenge through it is most revealing. The humour, the pathos, the determination, the tears and the triumphs are all here, not just in the big chapters, but in the details revealed through sentence and observation as Lydia's writing takes us with her, on this remarkable escapade across the USA.

The fact that this east to west ride across Route 66 was in aid of raising funds to support a cancer charity is not lost amongst the descriptions of life alone on the road, with only a bike for company, and a million and one challenges to overcome on a daily basis. The character analysis leaps from the pages.

It is a book not only destined to inspire cyclists and cancer survivors but human endeavour in all walks / rides of life.

Love hope and strength.

Mike Peters

Chapter 1 - Lowest of

lows....

So I had shaken hands with 2 strangers as they handed me my bike from the back of their car. Relieved to be safe, tired but also wishing today hadn't happened. I crawled into a really nice room, ordered dominos, plugged in all electrical kit and then set about catching up with facebook and emails whilst mentally bashing my head against a brick wall over and over. One voice in my head said.. 'it was only 20 miles and you probably covered that in the detour anyway, and on a rest day you can go out and do the 20 miles...' the other voice was the one doing the bashing! So I sat down to tell all, no hold barred, and hope that disappointment isn't your main feeling.....and here I am, hoping that having read that you will continue to read to discover how and why....

Possibly the lowest point of my whole journey, one which began a year ago with the words 'maybe I'll cycle across America'. How I found myself in the middle of Missouri, in the dark and with all options run out except for one, is a story told through blogs from the road. A story of headwinds and fatigue, friendship and panniers full of Love hope and Strength.

It begins with the inspiration of a man known to most of us as MP, the music he has written and the example he sets. Mike Peters, a founder of the charity that I cycled for and The Alarm, is currently being treated for leukemia and yet has more energy and passion for life than most of us could ever dream of having. His charity, Love Hope Strength Foundation is changing the way bone marrow donors are recruited around the world and the Rocks events have raised money to build cancer centers and provide much needed equipment to the communities in which they are held. It is because of his example that I set out on October the 4th 2013, with the aim of cycling Route 66 in a month, to raise as much money as possible and spread the word of Love Hope Strength wherever I could.

But first a bit of background......

Chapter 2 - I've been North South East and West in my Life...

In order to help you understand how I have become so crazy as to want to attempt something as big as cycling Route 66, in may help to know a bit about me, maybe it will even make it clearer in my own mind how I came to be the person I am.

An early influence on the way I have turned out was the books I read when I was younger. As soon as my dad judged that I was old enough he began passing on his collection of war books to me... Colditz, The Great Escape and the Long Walk formed part of my childhood education. Stories of courage and tests of physical and mental strength. Before long I was reading every book I could get my hands on about WW1, WW2 and the Vietnam war and this in time led me to the choice of the Royal Navy as a career... flying helicopters.

My love of the outdoors I think comes from my mum. Nature books and programs were also part of my upbringing and David Attenborough was practically a god in our house. That combined with yearly trips to the beautiful land that is Switzerland, with walks up to glaciers and through forests gave me my love of the outdoors and letting a part of it into your soul.

The dream of serving in the Navy stayed with me until the end of my school days when I applied and was accepted for a place at Dartmouth Royal Naval College. But there was a hitch. Despite passing my pilot's tests with good scores, I had been refused the opportunity to learn to fly due to what I called a technicality in my eyesight test. This was not before I had the chance to fly both a Robinson 22 (tiny helicopter) and a Sea

King (large helicopter) and scare myself stupid with the Dunker training (being lowered into the water, strapped into a helicopter pod and having to make your way out). I accepted a warfare scholarship and set off for Dartmouth, away from home for the first time in my life.

Dartmouth ... what can I say... everything you imagine a naval college to be, it was. Up at 5 am for PT.... running around from then until 8pm. Parades, inspections and the like. On reflection, I think I was too young, my heart was not totally in it and I was not the person I am today. It was tough and I think I gave up. A fact that I am now slightly ashamed of. Following basic training, I decided I had had enough and bought my way out to find myself back in Reading with no idea what to do with my life. I had met the man who was to become my husband and wanted to stay in the area. Despite not enjoying much of my experience at Dartmouth, I still didn't want a job that was predictable... no 9-5 for me that was for sure. Whilst I was deciding, I went back and worked at the cattery where I had had a summer and weekend job.

Three careers seemed to fit the bill.. Police, Fire service and Nursing. Frankly I chose Nursing because I could stay in Reading and it paid a bursary. So once again I started studying and settled into a home life which included 2 lovely step-children. I didn't hugely enjoy my nursing training until I had a placement on the neonatal unit.

Have you ever gone somewhere and felt that this is where you belong? Well I had at that point and when I finished my training - the neonatal unit was the only job I applied /begged for. Fortunately for me they were desperate for nurses and gave me a job. To be honest if they hadn't - I would have quit and at the age of 23 gone in search of my third career!

So that's where I have stayed and I could't have found a better place... (I'm honestly not just saying this because my colleagues are probably reading this). My job of a Neonatal Nurse Practitioner provides me with a challenge, friendship, family and the chance to occasionally make a difference in a small life.

And now to the other part of my life... The Alarm and Love Hope Strength.

I explain in my blogs how I came to hear of The Alarm and Mike Peters so I won't repeat what I say later. I lost the music for a while in my life as I was working and involved in family life. I think I lost part of who I was, or maybe part of who I wanted to be and although I have no regrets about that part of my life, when I separated from my husband, my mid-life crisis hit early and I decided that life was too short and set about finding myself again... ok big cliche i know but bear with me...

A New Chapter in the Book of my Life....

It was at that time that Music returned, in the form of The Alarm playing in Reading... I went, was mesmerized and found myself booking to see them again.. and again...

Mike Peters is one of two people who have inspired me in my life to reach out for my dreams and give everything to achieve them. He leads by example and has more energy than most people put together, and it is this energy and drive that has led him to set up Love Hope Strength Foundation all whilst battling cancer himself. On top of this he is also one of the most genuine people I know. Whilst watching The Alarm, I became aware of the charity and the cause it promotes and over the last few years have become more and more involved, meeting people who are now good friends along the way. Since February this year we have been able to swab people to register them for the bone marrow donor list and it has been a privilege to be involved in this and spreading the word.

So why the challenges... I mentioned my love of reading about adventure and courage... well this had grown and now in addition to war books, my shelves are filled with non-fictional accounts of climbing mountains, cycling around the world and Arctic adventures. In short anything about a physical and mental challenge or stories of defying the odds. These books made me ask questions about myself.. could I keep going when I was too cold,or too tired?. At what point would I give up if faced with impossibilities? What sort of person would I find myself to be? Would I have been the one to give up and die or the one who kept going? Memories of Dartmouth and running away from difficulties were still in my subconscious and it was hard to shake thoughts like this.

I can't run and I can't swim well, but I can cycle and though not particularly fast, I was at a point where 40-80 miles was not unreasonable. Trips mountain biking in Wales and the Peak District had become essential for the preservation of my sanity, in so much as I found in myself a need to get away from daily life and people and spend quality time with myself, out in the middle of nowhere. So I began to combine this with raising money for the charity. Mountain biking South to North Wales was the starting point, followed by a road trip from Snowdon (after Snowdon Rocks) to Ben Nevis, in time to participate in Ben Nevis Rocks. It was there that the idea for Route 66 was handed to me and the planning began!

Chapter 3 - It's gonna be a good year...

Shortly after I returned from Ben Nevis I received a message from someone asking if I was planning to do anything in 2013 and could he join in. I replied with the idea about Route 66 and soon firm plans were being made.

An awful lot of preparation goes into a trip like this and it seemed like a huge undertaking that got bigger by the second. Once there was a second person on board, it seemed reasonable to start thinking about a support vehicle and the possibilities for sponsorship. Now if anyone hasn't tried to get sponsorship for something, let me tell you, it's a lot of hard work, time and e-mails for little reward. Many of the companies I contacted wished us well in our endeavors but couldn't help. Other companies had already divided their charity/sponsorship budget for the coming financial year by December, leaving me drawing a huge frustrating blank on help with a vehicle.

It quickly became clear to me that for a support vehicle to be there, it would have to be self-funded and this would dramatically increase the amount spent. This was not my only concern. A training ride, in Wales with my partner in crime, showed that he was on the much fitter end of the scale than I was, which gave me worries about keeping up and not letting the side down.

Route planning also took up a great deal of my spare time. I was keen to plan the best route possible, keeping to the old Route 66 as much as possible. It quickly became clear that in order to complete this in 4 weeks (the maximum time I could take off work) we would have to cycle roughly 100 miles per day. I factored this in to route planning and even mapped out every day separately.

Then there was kit to think of. Buying bikes here seemed most feasible as it would mean we could break them in prior to the trip, getting used to the handling. With a support vehicle, this meant we could buy fast light road bikes as all kit would be in the vehicle.

Then just as I was about to book flights... the bombshell hit! My cycling buddy for this challenge was unable to participate. My first thought was, well there goes the support vehicle. I knew I couldn't afford it on my own and didn't know anyone who would be able to give 4 weeks of their time, let alone want to trawl after me at 15 miles an hour!! It also had repercussions on the type of bike I wanted.. but more of that shortly.

Once the dust had settled and my thought processes had digested this information, my second and third thoughts were that actually it might be better by myself, no one to keep up with and freedom to choose when and where I stopped and for how long. Add to that the thought that strangers are more likely to chat to and assist solo cyclists and I was feeling much better about the whole thing.

I then had to make a few phone calls... one of the conversations went like this.

Me: He pulled out of the ride...
Them: I'm sorry, maybe you could try again next year?
Me: Oh don't be, I'm still going: In fact I'm pretty happy with it...
Them: ....(silence)................ you what?

And so began a series of explanational conversations about how I would stay safe and well which led to the acquisition of

SPOT, a personal tracker with an SOS function, that could e-mail 10 people with a message (to say that I was ok) and the coordinates of my location.

SPOT wasn't the last piece of electrical kit I acquired and soon I was faced with a problem of maintaining charge on all these items... cue the purchase of a solar panel charger!

The tablet I bought came with an app for offline mapping and a GPS function so that I could pinpoint my position and reduce the chances of getting hopelessly lost. I almost lost this for good however when experimenting with a handlebar mounting. the bike hit a bump, the tablet jumped off, smashed face down on the road and avoided being pulverized by the wheels of a car by inches. Needless to say, I decided that I would just have to keep getting it out of my rucksack.

And so the preparations went on and on, each outing on my bike presenting me with another possibility for improvement or tweaking of details. Meanwhile plans were underway to experience the states on a couple of familiarization trips...

Under the heading of 'You only regret the things you don't do' I found myself on a plane to America for the first time, heading to Boston, where I would pick up a car and head to Rhode Island. I was going to see Joe Silva - a great musician and a friend of mine, play at a benefit for a young child with cancer. My excuse was to practice driving on the wrong side of the road. I couldn't really employ that excuse when only 3 months later I found myself on another plane, this time to Colorado. Here I managed to squeeze in a Big Country gig in Denver, swiftly followed by a walk up Vail mountain with LHS and Mike Peters. Here I made many new friends, and met up with already made friends, some of whom I would see again in November at the End of ride gig. Here also I was given the prayer flags which travelled with me along my journey along Route 66.

The idea of the prayer flags originated from Tibet, where legend has it that blessings get sent to those whose names are inscribed on the flags. The wind blows the flags and threads blown off from the flags are carried with the blessings to those people. Many people in Vail wrote names on the flags to be carried up the mountain that day... but I did not as an idea was forming in the back of my mind. Why not offer those people kind enough to sponsor me for my cycle ride, the chance to add a name to the flags? Not only would blessings be carried to these people but they would also make the journey with me. Little did I know how important these flags would become to me.

Time rolled past... bloody quickly as it has a habit of doing, and soon I was getting to the point where I had to decide on a bike. In my head, I knew it had to be sturdy and reliable. In my heart I wanted it to be fast and light. Many hours of deliberating and 2 bikes in the shop for viewing later...

My head won. And it is not a decision I regret. Much as a light fast bike would be great (for rolling around southern England), it would not have been the appropriate choice. so I settled on a Dawes, a good British make, with a pannier rack already fitted. I made a few changes for the good of the trip. I swopped the tyres for slightly thinner ones (and therefore lighter) and changed the pedals to clip in ones.

My other task was to promote my bike ride in order to get people to sponsor me for this crazy undertaking. Risking embarrassment and laughter, I even did a promotional video, complete with soundtrack, written, played and sung by myself. The video itself was shot using my tab, balanced precariously on the back of my rucksack whilst I cycled along. Although I didn't factor in the angle of shot, the resulting images of the trees and sky rolling past, created a video that suited the song and the ride. This video can be viewed using the following link:

http://www.youtube.com/watch?v=Dn5vcq0cNQU&feature=c4 -overview&list=UUD3m5jMvqSzjKP66kue7gUA

Then before I knew it October had arrived and there was nothing else left to prepare. All that was left was to pack, get on the plane and make my actions speak louder than all the words spoken about it..... At least that was the plan.

What follows is a day by day account of the highs and lows of the road as I experienced it. Apart from correcting the (many) typos, it is as I wrote it then. Anything I have added is in *italics* to distinguish between thoughts of then and now. I am not a professional cyclist and probably didn't train as much as I ought to have done prior to leaving. I am stubborn and hate the thought of anything beating me. I like a challenge and seeing where my limits lie. I am not the first to have done this and will not be the last and I couldn't have thought about attempting this without the support of family and friends.

Chapter 4 - The Road to Route 66 - Gale force winds and Love Hope Strength

I wanted to blog about the weekend I have just had for several reasons. Firstly to try and give people an idea of why I have become so involved with Love Hope Strength Foundation, to show you some of the things the charity does to raise money and to continue with my tale of fitness preparation for Route 66.

Ben Nevis Rocks - one of the events where people who support the charity, Love Hope Strength Foundation, come together, walk a mountain, and raise money and awareness for the charity.

What the above doesn't tell you is how I have made lifelong friends along the way and shared an experience that is difficult to put into words.

So the weekend began after a night shift - racing home and getting there just in time to find Steve ready to shove all the swabbing kit into his car to start the journey up to Scotland. On the way we swung by to pick up my step-daughter Anna, who was about to experience not only the mountain for the first time but also her first Rocks event. Then onwards and upward - eventually getting through the traffic - to Glasgow to pick up Brian. Steve is a dedicated volunteer who I have bumped into during a lot of Alarm/Big Country/Rocks events over the last few years. Brian I met on Ben Nevis last year and it seems like we have been friends for a long time. With such good company, the journey flies by, but we do arrive late to the pre-rocks gathering of walkers. However the scenery of the A82 made it all ok!

We headed off to our campsite, set up the tents and prepared for an early start!

03:30 to be exact and by 04:30 we were starting to gather at the base of the climb.

It was at this point that Mickey arrived. I shared the walk down Ben Nevis last year with Mickey and I think it is safe to say that we have become firm friends. So much so that the madness has rubbed off on him and he cycled from his home in Lochmaben to Ben Nevis - a distance of over 250 miles - to raise money for Love Hope Strength Foundation in memory of his brother Stevie. As they say in Cycling - Chapeau Mickey! He and his family raised a grand total of around £5000. Mickey is a good example of the kind of people that I was lucky enough to share the weekend with.

We then got treated to a song from Mike Peters, the founder of the charity and inspiration to many of us - before setting off in the dark, head torches on - up the mountain. It was cold and wet and the wind was such that the chill of the night air reached the bones pretty quickly but we all had smiles on our faces and before we knew it the daylight arrived. Anna set off at quite a pace, although not as fast as Mickey who practically ran up!

The walk provides us all with an opportunity to catch up with old friends and make new ones and if you have the tendency to think philosophically like I do sometimes - it is one of the few times when I can say that everyone present was there to do a good thing which is one of the reasons why I find it life - affirming in a way. It confirms that there are a lot of genuinely good people out there who will give up time and effort to do something for others.

However this year the mountain decided to throw all it had at us. It got so cold near the top that people's hands were swelling up (my knuckles have only just been found), extremities were numb, and if you took your hat off - brain freeze (as my step daughter so aptly put it) followed. then the wind made itself known - lets just say that if the wind can blow an adult off their feet - it's gotta be gale force.

This meant that time at the top was curtailed but am proud to say that Anna made it up there and didn't give up when it got tough. We managed a few lines of a song and a photo with Mike Peters before setting off at a reasonable pace - with the knowledge that the quicker we descended the quicker we would warm up. NB - tying up shoelaces with numb hands is an interesting exercise!!

Post the climb, when we all got back, we headed to the campsite to dry clothes, and get ready for the post-climb gathering!

This is where the swabbing comes in...

So we set up a stall and signed people up to the bone marrow donor list, it's easy and takes just 5 minutes of your time and you could help save a life!
Once again Anna made me proud by learning how to GET PEOPLE ON THE LIST and jumped in to lend a hand along with the other volunteers. 23 people signed up to the list, which was a great result.

Then the music - Mike was fantastic as people shouted out songs that he hadn't played for years in some cases but after a few seconds of thought, off he went and entertained us with his guitar that people had signed on the way. The Deceiver, True Life, The Message, 68 Guns to name but a few. Mike was kind enough to get me up to tell people about the bike ride - and following that I was blown away by the support of people who I had just met who were kind enough to donate and offer their support in this crazy challenge.

All good things must come to an end however and too soon it had all wound down. The stall was packed up and we are all left to reflect on how a group of people, many of whom didn't know each other before can all get on so well, and create a 'magical thing' (for want of a better way to describe it).

So I probably speak for all of us when I say to Mike and Jules, thank you very much for a wonderful weekend. Let's do it all again sometime soon!!

(SNOWDON ROCKS takes place next weekend!)

Snowdon Rocks was also a fantastic day... The weather was much better than Ben Nevis and there is a cafe halfway up. Always a bonus. Got to reconnect with different LHS friends and once again we had a successful swabbing venture. More people on the list = more lives potentially saved. the only drawback was somehow I had injured my foot - a problem that would persist throughout my ride. As I write this I have had an X-ray and am waiting for the results. It wasnt made any better by jumping up and down on it at Big Country gigs but having had a few days of complete rest.. it is now feeling much better!

Looking back on Ben Nevis, it seems to have been the first experience of ' nothing worth having is easily won'. It was possibly the worst weather I have climbed a mountain in, yet that only made the feeling of friendship and togetherness greater, and my pride in my step-daughter higher! I also want to point out that I am not the most crazy person that climbed the mountain. Nicola had decided to do 20 burpees at the top to gain some extra sponsorship. So it was because of her that I found myself counting upwards from 1 to 20, flinging myself down to the cold hard ground in an attempt to support her challenge. Unfortunately we were being filmed... fortunately the weather was so bad that you can only see the outline of us, jumping up and down with David's laughter for company.

Chapter 5 - Now for the last minute things...

So the week of the bike ride is upon me. My last day of work for a month is done and I have 2 days in which to panic efficiently and get everything done.

What is left to do you ask.... surely everything is sorted by now? And yes most things are done. 9.6kg of kit however and I am still not happy. Surely I could do without that extra pair of socks. Do I really need 5 packets of ibuprofen.... or if I took out the 'just in case' 2nd adaptor... or cut the end off the toothbrush (yes touring cyclists do do that to save 1 g)

So tomorrow one of my first tasks will be to go through the kit again and justify every single kg of weight.

Next up will be packing my bike in the box, ensuring that all remotely breakable parts are encased in bubble wrap and the box is secure.

Then I think double checking my passport, money, travel insurance and paperwork comes high up the to do list.

The other advantage of keeping myself busy over the next 2 days will be less time to dwell on what ifs. I have planned for as much as I can and the rest will be a case of reacting and dealing with issues as they come up. There is an endless list of things that could happen but I cannot, as in life, prepare for every eventuality. If we had no surprises in life, it would be boring, and with traveling it is much the same.

Sometimes the unexpected happenings are where we find the most enjoyment, learn the most about ourselves or experience something that changes us forever.

The only real worry I have is whether I will be up to the task. But whatever happens you can be sure I will break myself before I give up and try to be worthy of all the kind and generous people who have shown their support by donating, sharing my page and blog and in some cases going the extra mile to keep me positive!

So now that is said I thought I would share a funny, well according to everyone else anyway, story. The background to this is begins with a course at work which involved me coming up with a plan to implement a change. Mine involved getting my long suffering colleagues to walk up the stairs (all 6 flights) to work for 6 weeks. I wasn't very popular I can tell you. This was all part of my long running, formerly unofficial campaign to get everyone fitter.

So with this in mind imagine my upset, dismay, and general feeling of a dagger to my very soul, when it was suggested that should I die on this trip (I'm not planning to btw) they would dedicate, with a plaque, in my honour.... A LIFT!   cue huge amounts of laughter from everyone, except myself!

So watch out for my daily blogs, photos and snippets of life on the long dusty road called Route 66!

Looking back on this - I did not pack adequately. Next time I will not believe the weather forcasts and will pack at least 1 longer pair of cycling shorts! I think also there were many items of kit that I did not need. However I think taking the tent was a worthwhile back up plan and would take it again -

despite the fact I didnt use it, there were several occasions where it became a close possibility.

The tools and spares were a must have but much of the first aid stuff I didnt need and could have bought if necessary. Oh well - you live and learn right?

Chapter 6 - The time for talk is done...

So sitting at heathrow waiting for baggage drop to open to get my bike safely on it's way to Chicago and I thought I'd update about the last minute stuff.

Yesterday was a whirlwind... started off my dropping into work to say bye to my friends and those who are as close to being family as you can get without actually being.

Coulda been a mistake. The number of times I said 'I will be fine' cannot be counted on 2 hands and actually I didn't feel fine. If you know me you know I have energy to spare, now picture inside my head .... 10 thoughts rattling round every second... did I pack that.... do I need that.... what if.... help... am I really crazy... will I complete this.... will I let myself down.... cant wait to see the sign on the pier.... etc etc etc. Managed to keep this well hidden, to reassure all the people worried about me but it exploded the moment I got home.

The pacing started. Even as I made phone calls to some people who have been legends in their support for me I was pacing the floor... wound up as tight as a coiled spring. If I could have got in the car then and there I would have.

Even going climbing didn't help, my head wasn't in the game, or this planet which makes climbing difficult to say the least.

The afternoon passed in a haze of caffeine... another mistake. As if the nervous energy and adrenaline weren't enough, try adding lots of coffee to the mix... recipe for disaster.

By the time I got to my parents, I felt physically sick. Food didn't appeal in the slightest. And so the evening passed. Home, fed the snakes and a couple of hours kip later... Emma arrived to take me to Heathrow.

And so now, sitting at Heathrow, a year after Sandra sowed the seed of this crazy plan at Ben Nevis Rocks, I find myself completely calm.

Maybe its the fact that I'm sleep deprived, or maybe it's the knowledge that I cant do anything now if I have forgotten anything, there is no turning back....

The time for talk is done.... Santa Monica here I come!

Last minute nerves is inevitable and this was the longest cycle ride I'd ever done. I think next time will be easier!

At the time I didn't really pause to think about the effect me leaving to cycle in America would have on some of those that I know. It took me by surprise just how worried people were. I guess the difference is that at any given point of the day I know I am alright because I am with me... (I am making sense I promise), but people at home had to wait for SPOT or facebook before they could be certain that I was ok. At any rate - all the worry made it pretty hard to walk away. It seems like a hugely selfish thing to do in many ways but I hope they feel that it was all worth it.

Chapter 7 - Arrival in the Windy City

Well, the plane didn't crash so that is one less thing for everyone at home to cross of their worry list. I had arrived safely in Chicago. Its actually the 3rd time this year that I have been to the us so imagine my relief when they didn't invite me into the interview room at the border to explain that I wasn't running drugs from Europe, although a certain person did tell me that the picture of my bike in the box had some suspicious packages in it.

Because of my previous 2 visits I was quite familiar with the security process to enter the us, and my fingerprints are now on record for the 3rd time, but this time I didn't get the surly, don't smile or I will lock you up, border guard, instead I had a nice chat about my bike ride, including the by now familiar look of horror accompanied by the words "by yourself".

But this time it was followed by "awesome!". Yup, I was really in the U.S.A.

So next I went over to baggage claim, fingers and toes crossed that my bike had been put on the right flight and it was in one piece, both wishes came true and in no time at all, I was in the arrivals hall, putting my bike back together again.

Frankly this was a lot easier than getting it in the box and in no time at all I was outside the terminal, looking at the traffic coming from the wrong direction and working up enough courage to bite the bullet and go for it. Deep breath and off I pedaled, talking to myself as I went... keep to the right, left lane on the right, can turn right at a red light, oops need to change lanes. .... making sure I looked over my left shoulder instead of my right one took a bit of getting used to but I discovered that it all fell into place pretty quickly, my confidence grew and I found myself grinning from ear to ear as I started to enjoy.

I was making good speed 14 to 16 mph, there was weirdly no wind in the windy city, which suited me fine and it was if anything slightly too warm!
Merrily I biked along, remembered to look left and eventually came to where the GPS said I had arrived at my cousins, only to find out that there was no number 2222 and that my phone didn't want to call anyone here. But more of that later.

So thanks to the Garmin edge I borrowed (big big thanks to Matt) I realised after about 30 mins of panic that I could just program in the address and use like a sat nav. I do know that it took me a long time to do this but I was quite tired by this point.

So another few miles of good speed and I actually arrived.

Brilliant to see my cousin and her family who I hadn't met before and hadn't seen her for over 10 years I reckon.

So the phone, well my plan was to buy a sim card and fit into my phone, but a visit to a slightly dodgy repair shop told me that it wasn't unlocked and I couldn't so we went to a Wallgreens (pretty cool shops these, they sell pretty much everything), and bought a cheap phone. The saga continued when at the house, after a quick trip to the very cool local brewery, (where for the second time in the 30 min shopping trip I got told my hair was cool btw) and also took the opportunity to drop off some of my cards advertising my ride thee., (just realised this is a very long sentence) , and it then took an hour to set up the phone, as I couldn't find the phone number on the sim like in the UK but had to register online first.

But that got sorted and I am now the proud owner of an American mobile number !

So that was my day. 24 hours of being up and traveling and still making sense when speaking.
Just about..........

Thinking about the moment of actually setting off on my bike... It took about 10 minutes to work up the nerve to get going. I did feel pretty overwhelmed by the whole thing at that point. It was feeling as though if this bit didn't go well, the whole journey would be doomed... ok so that's quite ridiculous but in those few minutes that's what it was. But as with anything, the longer you think about something, the worse it gets. The business of cycling on the 'wrong side' of the road was fine after about 10 minutes...it was when I came back to the UK, when I found myself making a turn (fortunately on a quiet road) onto the Right hand side that I realised how quickly I had become indoctrinated to the US way of things.

The US mobile was invaluable throughout as my phone from home flatly refused to ring any number, so at least I was able to keep in touch with people in the USA.

'Don't think, just do.' (disclaimer: This only applies to things that have been previously well thought out and planned - I am not advocating leaving the house now on a month long cycle trip with no preparation!)

Chapter 8 - Day 1: It's alright to dream...

What I'm gonna try and do is take you on a virtual journey, so that you get what living life for a month on a cycle tour is like.

The day really started at half 6, and following a much needed shower I began to get my kit together. Water bottles were filled, my new phone checked and panniers attached. Prayer flags on the back etc. It all took a lot longer than planned so didn't set off till 8am ish. Now cycled along the lakefront a few miles, just to get to the start of the ride, the Buckingham fountain.

I stood by the fountain for photos, taken by my cousin's husband Matt, who was seeing me safely out of Chicago, and as I stood there, still not quite believing that this was it, I felt deliriously happy with life and everything in it. In bike riding you need to recognise and cherish these moments cos 10 mins later you might be feeling the worst you have ever felt in your life. If this was how I felt at the beginning, imagine how its gonna feel in L.A!

So the first few miles were punctuated with stops for photos but in general good roads, not too much traffic and feeling ok. Got through the south side without getting shot at and then that moment came where I was on my own. It wasn't long before I got into the swing of things and soon had stuck my music in an ear and was merrily singing to myself.

Having had a banana for breakfast, the first hunger pangs didn't hit till later. It was fluid I needed. It was hot and humid and I had a base layer on and no way to decently take it off, so the sweat was soon pouring.

About 40 miles in I hit the proverbial wall and stopped at a 7 eleven to stock up on lunch
The chocolate was a mistake as it soon melted but the roll hit the spot and I was soon on my way. It took a while to get on the right road but eventually got there and set myself up for the straight shot down to Joliet and then Dwight.

It was a straight shot but proved to anything but easy.

It was about 3 that the thunderstorm complete with lightening started. Now Illinois Is pretty flat and at points I was the tallest thing around, wearing shoes with metal cleats and on a metal bike. I did wonder how likely I was to be struck by lightening and although the rain was at first welcome, the fear made me pedal faster. It was just as well I did cos just as I arrived at a gas station, the heavens opened, and I'm talking about a flood the road in a minute flat kinda shower, so I stayed put and waited for it to pass. Cue nice lady who offered me shelter in her car! I didn't take her up cos even getting in a car seemed like cheating! But it was a lovely thought.

The road from then on was reasonable with a good hard shoulder and the lorry drivers have been, so far, far more considerate of the space they give to cyclists than most lorries back home. It gave me a sense of 2 things, firstly how its going to be for a lot of this journey , road stretching out before me with peace and solitude and the odd car, and just how distances on maps can be deceiving. I got to Joliet and thought not far to go, when actually another 30 miles was there to be suffered. And suffer I did. The legs felt ok at this point, it was the arms, the back, the bum, and the foot, which I thought I had broken last week that hurt.

UNTIL 4 MILES TO GO.Those 4 miles were amongst the worst I had cycled ever. But strangely I gained a kinda masochistic pleasure outta it. Endurance is meant to hurt, right?
Some lovely views were passed including a lot of Route 66 stuff and photos were taken but it took a long time till I reached my bed for the night.
I was born to burn down the road, its just going to be burning slowly at the end!

So highlight of the day... the start of the ride
Weight on starting , 68 kg (after carb loading last week
Food eaten, banana, roll, 2 x protein bars and home cooked chicken
Time crashed out........

Okay Okay so I admit, I probably didnt eat enough and that may be partly why I felt awful here. That and the lack of training prior to leaving. Looking back at this day- it wasn't that tough compared to some of the later days. Towards the

later stages of the ride I was much better prepared food wise and much more strict with myself about eating regularly. Some days it helped, some it didn't feel as though it did.

I find it difficult to eat lots as I never feel hungry out on long bike rides. Even in the evenings I could barely work up the energy to eat a whole meal. I thought I would immediately feel hungry the moment i got back home, but food still isn't a high priority - although the thought of Dominos tonight is a fairly good one!

Trouble is the time spent eating can be put to better use....

The moment when I was suddenly on my own actually hit me as hard as the moment outside the airport. It was that kind of ' well this is it' moment. Once again I took about 5 minutes to get myself 'organised' when actually during that time I was taking lots of deep breaths, mentally reassuring myself and generally keeping down the feeling of ... how to describe.... not panic or fear.. just a slight hollow feeling in the pit of the stomach and if I had been superstitious, this would have been the moment I touched some wood for luck.

Chapter 9 - Day 2: Every turn of the pedals is one step closer to L.A...

So my aim this morning was to set off about 8am. This plan was ruined by being awake at 4am so annoyed with myself I ended up leaving around 9am to blue skies. Nature must have seen my thoughts cos no sooner than I turned into the main road, I got hit, not by a rainstorm today but by the most dreaded thing of all, a strong headwind!

Let me explain what I discovered today. You hit a headwind here, not only is it strong but you are guaranteed to be headed into it for the WHOLE day.

If there is anything that can reduce a cyclists morale, its the knowledge that the next 80 miles are going to be tough ones, battling against the wind all the way. It can be so energy sapping that when the wind drops for a second or two, you are too knackered to take any advantage.

So my day consisted of this for all 80ish miles, with a few highlights thrown in.

And it is these highlights that must be dwelt on, otherwise I woulda been in pieces at the side of the road for sure. Before I go into detail about those, Roy asked me how I set my mind on a tough day.

Here is a list of strategies, some work better than others at any given moment

1. Music: always at the top of my list, especially when I can sing whilst going along. Hit the ground running, Swansong, Breathe and 1983/84 were at the top of my playlist today

2. Distractions: trying to look at the view instead of the speedometer

3. Ticking off the towns as I pass them

4. Remember why I am doing this in the first place

5. Thinking about the support from friends and family (this should be higher up the list)

6.Planning the next trip

7. Trying to remember that the pain is only temporary and in 10 hours it will have stopped

8. Thinking how good it will be when I get to the end

9. Determination not to let anyone down or let this beat me

So that's just a few and the emotions when on a bike ride can be so up and down, its like life has been squished to experience all emotions in as short a space of time.

Highlights of today include , seeing a woodchuck, or groundhog. Pretty cool

The young man who asked me where I was from and where going to, who was so amazed, that he bought me a coke and wished me luck. Its people like this that give u faith in humanity.

Seeing an original Route 66 bridge and reading the history behind it. Very cool.

Feeling really crap half way through, when Breaking Point came on my iPod and made me smile, cos I wasn't there, yet!

So my day got slightly worse when my sat nav ran out of battery. My back up was too but my solar charger did a grand job of keeping it up and running long enough to get out of bloomin normal, as I have decided to call it.

The last 40 miles were made even worse when my iPod died and due to my late start and the horrendous headwind, (so bad that if I stopped pedaling whilst going downhill, it blew me to a standstill), I was crawling along and it was getting dark. I had phoned my hosts for the night when I got to bloomin normal to let them know I was behind schedule and just as darkness started to fall, about 15 miles away from a bed, I saw coming along the road, 2 cyclists asking if I was Lydia. To my absolute joy and delight, these 2 people, who not only gave me a bed and food and hot shower use tonight had come to meet me to escort me to their home.

It was a lovely gesture, just when I had started pedaling squares, they provided companionship, shared stories of similar days on a bike and cheered me up no end.

So that was my day. Not as good as yesterday, possibly better than 1 further down the line, but at the end of the day, the pedals kept turning, I am still smiling and I am one step closer to L.A. and challenge completion! :)

I'm still amazed at the generosity of my hosts. Not many people would welcome a complete stranger into their home and go the extra mile to come out and find them. This does typify the cameraderie of cycling though. Most cyclists will nod to each other on the road, with a shared understanding.. whether it is because both are battling against crappy weather or both enjoying a perfect days cycling.

A bit more on mental distraction: Especially towards the end of the bike ride, I noticed that much of my time on the bike was spent mentally calculating mileage, time until dark, plans B and C if plan A didn't work and generally thinking about the basics - food and shelter. This happened more if the day was a difficult one and was like a survival instinct kicking in. On days where the wind was behind me or the gradient was good, more time was spent thinking about family and friends and homelife.

And then there was the singing - apologies now to anyone who heard me belting out Absolute Reality, I know it amused some of the cattle along the way!

Chapter 10 - Day 3: What a difference a day makes...

Whatever doesn't kill you only makes you strong,..... yesterday did not break me and so I awoke with fresh optimism and I would like to say full of bounding energy, but I still hurt all over so there was much less bounding.

Once again, woke up a bit later than planned after my what is now becoming my usual 4am sleep break but managed to get out by half 8, escorted once again by my host, who very kindly rode the first 12 with me.

It had been really nice to chat with people who understood the challenges of bike tours and they made me feel very welcome in their home.

Weather... started off with a mild headwind and overcast and I desperately tried to mentally prepare myself for 100 miles of hell. But actually, the sun came out and the headwind dropped and mixed it up between that, a sidewind and even occasionally a tailwind. So I managed to start enjoying the days ride, trogging along nicely at 14 mph until 20 or so miles later I reached Springfield... no I didn't meet Bart or Homer. Instead I found a lovely little town.

Springfield is one of the few places where I made a slight detour to sightsee. Lincoln's tomb is quite a magnificent thing and I stopped and did the tourist photos... in the process asked a lady to take a photo and turns out she was originally from Farnborough and will visit again next year. Had to happen at some point this trip right...

Following the tomb visit I was quite aware that I had used up valuable time and needed to motor somewhat. So put the metal to the pedal and aided by lack of wind, glorious sunshine, and warmth in my very weary bones I set off at a good crack and I reckon managed an average of 14 to 15mph if not higher, which is good going, especially when you have rolling roads. Traffic was kind to me and passed well to the side. Got a few waves and head nods to brighten my day and managed to enjoy the scenery, fields and fields of golden corn with the white silos adding to the perfect picture.

I motored on down, stopped at a gas station to check the route and was stopped by a lovely lady who asked me what I was doing and even asked for a picture. More nice strangers!

I eventually came to another town and prepared to go straight through when I was stopped in my tracks by a very picturesque, old square.

A courthouse where Abe had practiced used to stand there and I really got a sense of the history of the road I had been riding all day.

This was my last real stop before my destination. So the last 25 ish miles went by.. not without a sting or 2 in the tail. Almost got too friendly with a 4 x 4 whose driver didn't obey the stop sign on her side of the road as she was turning, seems arsehole car drivers do the same things the world over... got chased by dogs, not a first for me but always a little disconcerting... and the last few miles to the town were all up a reasonably steep incline. That said I stopped at the general store and asked where the motel was and they directed me the 2 or so miles to where I found a bed, shower, wifi and a Dairy Queen.

Now I have been here 3 days and haven't set foot in a Mac D's, but succumbed to a calorific cheeseburger which I am heartily regretting and a very nice, low calorie, fruit smoothy.

So I am tucked up, nice and warm reflecting on how hardship makes the most simple things great.

Finally, I don't want everyone to think today was a breeze so I thought I'd list the catalogue of aches and pains:

My knee is very stiff and hurt with every pedal turn for the first 50 miles

My back and shoulders hurt like hell

Sunburnt face, leg and neck... I did use sunscreen just not enough

Sitting down hurts

My left finger won't straighten, not sure whats wrong with it

My left foot is still possibly mildly broken

Is that enough....

So goodnight all. All is well on Route 66 for another day!

At this point I probably wasn't as worried about my fingers as I should have been. After nearly 2 weeks at home the Right 4th finger will not straighten and playing the guitar has been difficult to impossible. I have been reassured by the GP that it will improve and am given hope by the fact that the Left finger is pretty much back to normal. But it has been worrying me due to the fact that I need my hands to do my job - never mind anything else. Before I left I made a promise to someone not to break myself beyond repair... i wasn't thinking about use of my fingers at that point - it had never occurred to me that it might be a problem. I was thinking more of head injuries, smashed legs and the like.

Funny how it's always the little things in life that can make a difference for good or for bad.

Chapter 11 - Day 4: No one said it would be easy...

So I have had to do a lot of thought about what to write today... I feel like I have let myself and others down. But I figured that the best thing to do on this day of 3 parts was to start at the end and then go back to the beginning and let you make your minds up as to whether you agree.

Experience is merely the name men give to their mistakes...(Oscar Wilde) well I guess I gained a lot of experience then

Part 3- the end of the day

So I had shaken hands with 2 strangers as they handed me my bike from the back of their car. Relieved to be safe, tired but also wishing today hadn't happened. I crawled into a really nice room, ordered dominos, plugged in all electrical kit and then set about catching up with facebook and emails whilst mentally bashing my head against a brick wall over and over. One voice in my head said... it was only 20 miles and you probably covered that in the detour anyway, and on a rest day you can go out and do the 20 miles... the other voice was the one doing the bashing! So I sat down to tell all, no hold barred, and hope that disappointment isn't your main feeling.....and here I am, hoping that having read that you will continue to read to discover how and why.

Part 1- The beginning of the day

I woke, at 4am, as seems to be the pattern, dozed a little, but then got it together to aim for an 8am departure. Breakfast was handmade waffles, which was pretty cool and a reasonable cup of coffee. Packing up my stuff took a lot longer than expected so approx 8:15 I was on the road. Sun was shining, birds and crickets were singing, music in my ear and a good wind to guide me along at 15-16mph. I settled into a rhythm and no sooner than I had I saw an open Route 66 museum with the famous buried cars outside... I had to stop. Got some stuff as memorabilia and chatted with the owner who seemed to know about me (lol). Took lots of photos (see below) and chatted away.

Time flew past and I'd lost a good chunk of time, but it didn't matter cos the weather was good and I was feeling good. Back on the road and the towns whizzed by until my sat nav got slightly confused due to the fact that I was completing one planned day and starting the next. How did I find out that I was heading in the wrong direction? Not using technology that's for sure. In a moment of .. somethings not right, I looked at the sun and realised it was to my right and I was heading back North. Fortunately I realised before I had gone too far and it didn't take me long to get back on track. The miles whizzed by and at the same time as cautioning myself against it, I was feeling on top of the world!

I reached the outskirts of St. Louis at around midday, in good time ... and stopped for a while to admire the view (pic below).

The bridge was lovely, I could see for miles and I felt that I had bridged one hurdle.. this was the end of Illinois, shortly I would be in Missouri. This was also a symbolic place cos it is at this point that Route 66 turns westwards.

I felt quite reflective as I stood on this piece of history and marveled at all the chain of events that had led me to this point, good and bad in my life that meant I was nearly 300 miles in to a journey of a lifetime.

Part 2 - welcome to Missouri

St Louis itself, a city, generally I don't like them much anyway. I entered the city in what was probably a less affluent area. Stories of drive by shootings fleeted through my head, but only for an instant, because actually I felt pretty safe

The roads were wide and there were signs everywhere saying share the road with bikes, a good omen I thought. The university area was pretty and due to traffic and lights, it was taking a while to get through the city. So I continued on and stopped briefly at a very nice pub where I ordered a very very good sandwich!

The road out of St. Louis on Route 66 is highway 100. I'm not going to say much or dwell on highway 100, but even for a very confident cyclist, it was not a pleasant road and I don't think I would drive it again. That said, I got out of St. Louis safely and continued on.

I'm not sure where things went wrong but they must have at some point because although I was on a good, what seemed like a main road, in fact it wasn't, and a very hilly one at that too. It went up and down very steep sections, so much so that I had to walk up 2 hills cos the lowest gears weren't low enough. That didn't matter so much. What did matter was that due to the hell of St. Louis and Highway 100 it was getting late, and the hills weren't helping. Then I found a better road which took me back to the main road but at a price of more miles, hills and time. I wasn't worried or scared though. I had all lights blazing and was managing to freewheel fast enough down the hills to get most the way up the next (33 mph seems to have been my top speed) and I was doing it like the pros, head to the handlebars, bum in the air etc. I was even starting to enjoy myself again.

I got to a gas station on the main road and stopped to see how far away from St. Clair I was. 20 miles was the estimate, followed by ... you are not doing that in the dark are you? I replied they I thought I had to as there wasn't anywhere to stay around there. But actually I had made peace with the fact that I was going to be cycling in the dark, I would just be extra careful. Then someone else came up and said that he thought it was too dangerous as there wasn't really any hard shoulder, then a third gentleman came over and said pretty much the same thing and offered me a lift with my bike to St. Clair.

Now I know that I have been joking about plaques in the lifts at work, but having felt that I had dodged one bullet today (highway 100) and all these local people telling me it wasn't safe but there was no where to stay I made a decision that I do in many ways regret.

However it was that point that the words of a very wise person came to mind, who told me not to cross the line between broken and unmendable. I chose the hardest but probably the most sensible. I felt like I was 100 ft from the summit of Everest and had to turn back to ensure I made it down.

So that's the story of the day and I leave it up to you to make of it what you will.

The kind gentleman in the car said ' when you get to LA you won't care about the 20 miles' . I see what he is saying, however I think I will, so with that in mind I plan to, at some point do an extra 20 miles to complete the distance.

So now I m going to eat my pizza, shower, and prepare for a much much earlier start tomorrow, with no early distractions.

I am making use of my experience.

I can say this now... I was terrified coming out of St Louis.. I came pretty close to colliding with several cars, all of whom were speeding along, chatting away on their mobiles, not having a thought for any other road users out there. I would like to point out that I was LEGALLY cycling on this stretch of road, there was even a bike lane, not that it made the blindest bit of difference.

Yet despite all this i wouldn't have changed it one bit... yes I know I have a screw or two loose. Let me explain...

It was scary but at the same time I got the kind of adrenaline rush you get from bungee jumping (I'm guessing as I have never been). Skating a very fine line between life and (to put it bluntly) a box. And the feeling when I came out the other side of that road... life affirming I call it. Every sense is on hyper alert and life feels bloody good! (Apologies to everyone who feared for my life... last time I will say it... you were right!)

However Life is risk at the end of the day and I stand by my statement of 'to really live you have to put aside the fear'. Not that I'm recommending everyone fly out to St Louis for thier own taste of Highway 100, but instead try to do something you fear every now and again.. I think you will be surprised at your capacity to overcome it.

As for the 'lost' 20 miles.. I havent actually thought about it in the last 2 weeks so maybe the gentleman was right about it not making a big difference once I'd reached the pier. I do however remember how greatly appreciative of the support I received after this post I was. It was truly the lowest point of the trip and without all the kind words of family and friends, perhaps the rest of the trip would have been blighted by this one incident.

Chapter 12 - Day 5: I'm not going backwards... I'm only facing forwards

So I woke up earlier this morning, dusted myself off and with the help of all my friends and family stood back up, ready to face another day. A surprise phone call made the day already bright and managing to get myself together quicker, I was out and on the bike by 07:15 - apologies for the length of the blog today, I've got so much time to think and want to share every step of this journey.

The morning chill was fended off with several layers and as I set off a beautiful sight of mist and sunshine and trees seemed to be a pretty good omen for today.

The legs were given a rude awakening by the rolling terrain but it didn't matter cos I was in a good frame of mind and the view was lovely.

I had originally planned to aim for Lebanon at 118 miles but given yesterdays events I had researched places to stay and decided that I would go for slightly less today, and add it on to the originally planned 60 miles on day 6. So with this in mind , I was keen to get to Rolla by lunchtime and other than a few photos, kept on, through Sullivan and Bourbon. All was going well with no distractions when I rolled into Cuba, saw a sign for Route 66 fudge and squealed to a halt! Fudge aside, Cuba is a very pretty town, with an old Route 66 feel to it and I enjoyed spinning through. After Cuba, fresh determination not to stop until I reached Rolla would have gone well if it were not for the worlds biggest rockin' chair.

Once again my brakes issued smoke as I pulled in to admire. Whilst I was there I met a lovely couple who showed great interest in the ride and in chatting to them I was reminded that it is not just the destination, but how you get there that makes it a journey, and a big part of that for me is spreading the word about Love Hope Strength foundation and the great work that Mike, Jules, James, Shannon, Rob and all the volunteers do to help others.

Part of my rejuvenation today was reading Mike's blog from Israel, which if you are not already aware of LHS,, were you to read, you would perhaps understand why I became involved with the charity and why I am proud to be part of the LHS family (www.lovehopestrength.co.uk) . Reading it this morning helped find a renewed determination, that took a bit of a battering yesterday :)

So finally I left the rocking chair and continued westwards. I kept going until I hit the outskirts of Rolla, where just as Third Light (a Mike Peters song about loss in war), hit my iPod, I came upon a veteran cemetery. It seemed appropriate to stop for a few minutes reflection before caving into the inevitable...

yup.... Macdonalds. The free wifi made it worth while tho and I kept myself content with a small portion!

So time lost, but still feeling good about the day, as I followed the sat nav through Rolla obeying every instruction to the letter. I knew that the frontage roads did not go along all the way so a circuitous route was needed, however once again, a few miles later, I looked at the sun and got that sinking feeling. Another detour - prob 5 miles in total and using my offline maps and GPS decided to chance going back towards the interstate and frontage roads, whilst ignoring the sat nav pleading with me to do a u turn! So the detour obviously consisted of going back up that hill which I had merrily whizzed down but eventually I found myself back at the interstate and took a chance with the frontage roads, at least in the knowledge that navigation would be easier.

And so it proved to be, right up to the point where the frontage roads ran out both sides of the interstate, so I went to the gas station to ask what they thought best. The reply was not the best news I have ever had. There is a long way round.... prob a 30 mile detour, either that or the interstate. Cant I cross that river, I ask, with thought of wading up to my neck in cold stream water just to get to the next frontage road. Nope cant do that. Other people kindly weighed in with their thoughts... is it legal to ride on the interstate if there is no other way... apparently legal but not recommended came the reply,

Fair enough....interstate it is... deep breath.... and I needn't have worried... lovely road, generous hard shoulder, lorries gave me a wide berth, but dragged me along and I found myself grinning with the adrenaline rush of a 30mph jog along. Then back to the frontage road and a bloody great hill or 2 or 3. Shoulda stayed on the interstate!

That said, clearly this was an old part of Route 66 and crappy road surface maybe, but I was back in the tucked position, and took to saying free miles whenever the downhill was good (gotta amuse myself somehow!). That said I started to enjoy the rhythm of the uphill too and with the evening sun to boot, and little lizards running about everywhere life felt great. The worries of yesterday were eased, I had made good miles today, about 100 and arrived at a junction with motels and daylight to spare.

I managed to talk the receptionist into giving me a discount and get to stay tonight in a proper American motel! Pretty cool.

Dinner was grilled bacon, egg and cheese and a cup of coffee... tasted pretty good and I don't need to worry bout the calorie count today, but starting to crave fresh fruit!.

So time to check tomorrows route and motel placement, shower and pack for the morning,

And as I quoted this morning with breakfast.... this is life, its alright, its ok! X

Just to embellish on the story behind 'The World's Largest...'
When i was younger I watched a film called Michael... nice film about a road trip through USA with an Angel... bear with me...
Anyway on this road trip they made lots of detours to see 'The World's Largest Frying Pan' or 'The World's Largest Ball of String'. It coloured my impression of america and set up the story behind why I wanted to see 'The World's Largest Rocking Chair'.

The Interstate riding here was a gentle introduction to 'freeway' riding. It was pretty quiet and although there were some lorries it would be nothing like I encountered in California.

Finally for my comment on this day's blog, The motel I stayed at was one of many that kindly gave me discounts or upgrades throughout my stay, some without me asking. I guess they took one look at me and the state I was in and felt sorry for me!

Chapter 13 - Day 6: Embracing the randomness....

So day 6... having stopped earlier yesterday, my short day turned out to be another 90 ish miles. However I now have got leaving down to a fine art and managed to set off just as the sun was coming up. It was a bit chilly and I was glad of my layers. Today started off where yesterday finished with up and down roads. The first 30 miles saw my legs quietly screaming at me and no amount of shuffling around on my saddle could make that any better either. So settled in for a long day.

At 30 ish miles I came across yet another Route 66 gift shop and against my better judgement stopped. I say against better judgement cos I knew I'd walk out with something and anything I buy now has to be carried a few more miles. The other reason that it was a bad idea was the signposts

These signs were somewhat demoralising... yes I knew I had a ways to go but seeing the exact distance left to pedal, somehow made it more daunting. Up till now I hadn't considered really the next few weeks. My plan was always to get through the day that I was on. If I did that for 28 days, I would get there.

After this stop I vowed to keep going for another 30 before stopping again, and although the scenery was pretty, and In many places reminded me of home, it was hard to appreciate when you are struggling uphill, or trying to make use of the 'free miles'. which is what my entire day consisted of, up or down, no in between. All this time I was looking longingly at the interstate, which cut through the hills I was climbing. No wonder people think Route 66 is flat!

So because my day was just long and not hugely interesting, to amuse myself I devised a few informative lists:

List 1: Animals I have seen
Groundhog
Eagle (dead)
Armadillo x2 (both dead)
Tortoises x4 (flat and dead)
Skunk (I think, but dead)
Raccoon (dead)
Lizards (barely seen but alive, they move quickly)
Some kind of vole (also briefly)
Dogs x3 (as they are chasing me)

That's about it so far, would be nice to see something alive

List 2: Rules I have set myself for stopping
1. Never ever stop at the bottom of a hill

2. Don't stop in the middle either

3. When stopping unclip the foot nearest the pavement first

4. Don't forget to unclip the other foot as well

5. Try and stand over your bike, getting your leg back over following a stop is tricky

6. Try and combine stops with picture taking, eating, drinking whilst obeying rule number 5.

7. When leaving from your stop, do not leave your SPOT tracker lying on the top of the panniers (I forgot to mention THAT error yesterday)

8. Don't stop anywhere you hear dogs barking

9. One stop per hour or 10 miles, whichever comes 1st

10, never ever sit down! The muscles will have difficulty getting u back up again.

So anyway, I finally reached Springfield, Missouri to a warm welcome by a friend of a friend, whose company had kindly sorted out a place to stay... and not just any place. This hotel is somewhat different to the super 8 motels that i have been in so far and aside from feeling slightly out of place, its lovely so thank you very very much to Kelley, Shelley and the Austen Dooley company.

Having seen my bike safely in my room, I wondered over to the bbq place to eat. Forgetting about differences in portion size, I ordered a starter and some chips, only to struggle to eat a third of either. Whilst I ate I read a bit more of the book I downloaded, Extreme South about an attempt to the South pole and back. Aside from making me feel better about the struggles I face today, there were a few things that struck a cord with me.

Advice to them of ' eat before you get hungry, drink before you get thirsty, take off your jacket before you sweat and stop before you burn up 80 % of your energy' Good advice for any challenge. I agree with their query though. because of changing factors in any journey, how do you know whether you are too far short of your limits or whether by pushing a bit harder you will discover new limits and break personal boundaries. Interesting huh. I guess I might well find out over the next few weeks!

So that is about it for today. Hopefully tomorrow will bring similar success.

One day, one pedal turn at a time and I will make the next 1700 odd miles.

What I haven't really dwelled upon in this day's blog is just how uncomfortable I felt in this hotel. You see, there was me, in ripped shorts, covered head to toe in grime, in unwashed (for several days I might add) clothes with a bike - walking (in my equally grimy shoes) on polished floors, in glass elevators and surrounded by people in suits. Don't get me wrong - I'm incredibly grateful to everyone that enabled me to stay here and the manager was fantastic - see chapter 13 - but I did feel hugely out of place.

It has also occurred to me that I haven't updated my list of animals in my blog - so at the end is a comprehensive list of all wildlife that I stumbled upon.

Finally, though I have only mentioned a couple of books throughout these blogs, it is these and many others that have nurtured my crazy ideas of things I want to do and experience. Books like 'Into thin air', anything by Ranulph Fiennes or James Cracknell and a myriad of real life adventure stories have shaped my desire to experience the extreme depths of suffering for achievement. My little journey in no way compares with many of these tales - as I flaked out somewhat by electing to motel it every night!

But everyone begins somewhere... one day I will tell you about my 10 year plan to summit Everest (If I win the lottery). And although it doesn't compare - many of the aspects of planning and execution are the same for any grand scheme - first dream, then plan, then (most importantly) do!

Chapter 14 - Day 7: The only limitation is in my mind….

Just before I set off from my posh hotel, the general manager introduced himself and then gave me one of the hotels team jerseys... in good spirits I set off through Springfield with the wind behind me, singing along to Wonderful World... And it was. The miles flew past and the countryside began to subtly change... the hills were not as steep, there were less trees and life felt good.

You would think after 6 full days of biking I would know enough not to voice it out loud, or even whisper it....

So as I turned out of Springfield to once again head westwards... it started. Not headwinds this time, well at this point anyway, but sidewinds. Now if you have never cycled in a sidewind, just watch the tour of Belgium. Basically all the guys behind the one in front cycle slightly to the side for protection. I obviously couldn't do that, so instead I had to lean slightly into the wind to stop it blowing me off the side of the road... which worked well until I hit a road that had just been tarmacked... only they hadn't done the shoulder.

So picture this if you will... I'm hugging the white line, unable to go too far right as I will hit the gravel, and going any further left was out of the question.

This is tiring enough in itself... then factor in the lorries.

So lorries passing me, normally not a huge problem, they have generally given me plenty of room, but when they pass you when you are leaning into a sidewind and the sidewind suddenly disappears... well you get the idea, you get sucked in slightly, whilst trying to compensate, which then stops cos the lorry is past and then you get pulled forwards a little too... its like what I imagine being in a whirlpool is like.. before being spat out the other side..

So now you understand sidewinds and lorries and hopefully you get the picture of how much concentration is therefore required. And that was only 30 miles into a long long day.

This battling lasted for quite a while until the roadworks had finally finished and I got back my hard shoulder (yes I have become quite possessive of them). The sidewinds continued but at least I was managing a decent pace.

My other concern, was that in my joy of good wind in Springfield I had neglected to get any food for the day. Now although it wasn't critical, because I had a stretch of about 30 miles of nothingness only, it might well be crucial later on and better to get into good provision habits sooner rather than later.

Fortunately I hit a gas station reasonably quickly and loaded up on protein bars and the like. The road continued onwards, still battling against the sidewinds and 2 things occurred.

1. I saw a snake... yes it was dead :(.

2. I discovered that I actually HATE dogs. They seem to think it fun to chase me along the road, darting in close before trying to commit suicide under my front wheel. Now if you are not the one on the bike, you might find it quite funny... picture this.... always when the cyclist is at their slowest do the dogs strike, often in pairs, sneaking up behind them, as they cannot hear the warning barking cos of the wind whistling. Then its divide and conquer. While one distract the other darts in, narrowly avoiding the pedals. Meanwhile the cyclist is trying not to swerve into oncoming traffic, or be bitten by the one on the blind side. The cyclist shouts at the dogs whilst pedaling bloody fast to get out of their range. The dogs take absolutely no notice whatsoever, just missing the front wheel by inches.

If the owner is about they might decide to step in at this point, which is when the cyclist apologises profusely for swearing at the dogs.

If there is no owner, the dogs will continue the chase until well beyond the boundary of their territory before stopping, giving one last parting bark or growl and then trotting back for a nap.

The cyclist meanwhile is on the verge of collapse from trying to outrun the pack uphill and stops, possibly shaking slightly, not from fear, more from anger at the stupid dog owners who think it is acceptable to let their doberman, spaniel, husky (delete as appropriate) run around free.

Then multiply this incident by 3 for today and you see why I HATE dogs.

So where was I.... sidewinds yes... continued for much of the day, zapping me of all will to live, never mind continue. Then I hit Webb city. This was one of the most run down, desolate, horrible places I have seen so far. It has clearly suffered from degradation since I44 has been built and I was glad to get through it. Joplin quickly followed and with it the headwinds returned. Bit of relief from aching arm muscles but slow slow progress. I tried the trick of convincing myself that the 40 ish miles to go was just a short jaunt out for me, which back home it is, but every 10 miles had started to feel like 20. On top of that, I was determined not to add miles on to tomorrows ride by stopping short of my planned destination unless I absolutely had to and so I just kept going. Didn't feel hungry so didn't eat. Drank some but prob not enough. But conscious that I was just going to scrape in before it got dark.

Once through Joplin, the roads became more deserted and the dogs surfaced again. But then I hit Kansas. Now by this point I was soooo knackered I didn't actually care about any sights but thought I ought to take a few pics inside kansas just for the record. An old bridge and a pretty mural were the choices and both pictured below.

I would say I went so fast through Kansas I didn't notice it, bit actually it was painfully slow, dogged by the headwind again. And so it continued into Oklahoma... headwind, sidewind, headwind as I zigzagged south to Miami.

Just before Miami was my back up staying place, but as previously said, I was determined to get the miles done and still had an hour of daylight. I passed by the motel with an inward groan, knowing I was going to regret not stopping. And soon did...

The last 15 miles were tough. Not just tough but I think I had pushed my limits of endurance up to that point and then continued past them, so determined was I to get to Miami. 6, 3 2 miles to go. Everything hurt. Felt battered, broken, but was somehow still going. Not sure how.

Arrived in Miami just as sun going down, and then had to endure another 2 or 3 miles to find a motel. That was torture, to be so close to bed, shower etc and then have to go just a bit further...

Still less miles to do tomorrow...

The first motel I came to, I stopped at, looked so bad that they gave me a senior discount lol and then bought washing powder to do my laundry.. finally.

So there is no way around it, my clothes reeked, to the point that I couldn't stand myself. The bonus being that no one else had to stand it as well. But there are limits, even when doing this sort of thing, so did the laundry, whilst feeling a bit tired, crap, faint etc then ran (well limped) all of 20 feet to the sports bar for food... too tired to really eat and fed up of fast food, once again didn't finish the food. But then hobbled to my room, sat on the bed and started this blog.

Worried I pushed myself too far and will be broken for tomorrow. Have 2 more days to get through before that much needed rest day.

Wish I could say the day ended the same way it began, but today, the wind blew away my words and it is all I can do to whisper.... I'm so tired, take me now, come on and rescue me!

Nite all x

LHS

I just want to be clear about the subject of smelling awful...

I did shower every night - preferably before going out to dinner, where I would be in the vicinity of other people. It was only my clothes that smelt bad. Most people would be horrified at this but believe me, if it was a choice of wearing really stinky clothes or hauling another few kilograms of kit across 2400 miles, I know which one everyone would choose. Towards the end I was even contemplating chucking away 1 complete set of clothes in order to haul less weight - it was only out of respect for Beki and Randy, who were meeting me at the end, that I decided to keep a set of washed clothes for the last day.

I still warned them in advance though!

The most positive thing about this day, was that when blogging I obviously thought that i had overdone it, reached the limits of my endurance. Yet once again I am amazed at the potential of the human body to endure punishment in the form of physical exertion and more importantly of the mind to accept it!

Chapter 15 - Day 8: breathe the air: It's the only thing you get for free....

I didn't sleep well last night due to the bloody great big thunderstorm. I was concerned about cycling across flat land on my bike, basically serving as a lightening conductor. However the storm abated and I got up at 5 am to overcast skies and drizzle but not cold and no wind to speak of. Excited to make the most of this I packed up in super quick time and headed off to breakfast, to be told it was saturday and therefore breakfast not available until 7am. Such is life.

Once 7 am arrived, i jumped in for breakfast and was soon on my way. Despite it being overcast, the wind was for once with me and I shot out of Miami. The road was straight, reasonably flat and aimed in the same direction all day, rising to the belief that I would be enjoying a tailwind all day.

I had a few pressing issues, one of which I dealt with as soon as I found a shop. Disaster had befallen me last night as I reached Miami... my headphones had given up. I cannot, I repeat cannot cycle without music and on my spare headphones the sound of the alarm was more like, the sound of... well it might be the alarm but I couldn't tell u for sure. Fortunately the gas station sold headphones as well as guns, knives, and more pertinent to me, shots of energy juice. So loaded up with a couple of those just in case the day turned bad, and with working music again, i set off once more.

The road was wide and straight and i was able to enjoy the day. Looking at my surrounding, there were miles of fields and for the first time really since the trip began I had the pleasure of being alone on the road for stretches at a time.

For the first time, my mind could wander from the road to other things in my life... thoughts of home and family and friends that I miss, the dissertation I have to start when I get back (second thoughts, maybe too much time to think is a bad thing). My dog radar was kept on background alert but for once did not get set off at all.

I got to the top of a hill and the sun was starting to make itself felt, so I stopped to take off a layer or two and was confronted by a picture perfect view. I paused the iPod and just stood there... admiring the view, breathing the air and feeling lucky to be alive. It was one of those perfect moments that I find whilst biking, no distractions, no interruptions, just purity. This is why I came to America, for moments like this. A friend pointed out to me that you cant appreciate highs without experiencing the lows and he is totally correct. I'm not sure this moment would have been as appreciated if the last few days hadn't been rough!

Whilst standing there I noticed a white truck stop up ahead and then turn round and go back down the road... now because I am by myself I have a radar for things like this too and my internal warning system was on high alert. 2 mins later the truck pulls up to me. Staying where I was I asked if all was alright,

The reply I got was ' are you ok, are you lost, do you need help'. I replied that I was grand and felt really bad that I'd been thinking the worst. They then said we just wanted to check... I thanked them and they drove off, leaving me once again marveling at how nice people can be!

So once again I set off, the wind carrying me at a rate of knots. Now I mentioned the headphone problem and one I couldn't sort. Basically my hands don't work properly from gripping the handlebars for over 750 miles in 8 days. This makes things like attaching my iPod to my belt loop take up to 5 mins and you should see me trying to use a knife and fork... it is quite funny... as long as its only temporary, which it should be. One of my fingers, the forth on my right, will not straighten of its own accord. The other minor injury i have is my left foot. I injured it on snowdon somehow, possibly a stress fracture of one of the small bones. Whilst I am cycling along its fine... so actually all good, but today accidentally put that foot down at some lights and it really was quite painful, so just wont do that again. Other than that, a myriad of bruises, aching muscles and a bit of sunburn, actually i feel pretty good.

The road from this point to Tulsa cannot go by without me mentioning 2 more things... first is Spot, my companion for 30 miles (remember i have to keep myself entertained) Spot was a little bug who hitchhiked a ride, yellow with black spots (hence the name). He kept me entertained for a while, crawling around on my handlebar bag, looking like he was catching the bus to work! (No iIhaven't really lost it)

The other piece of entertainment i alluded to back in Missouri, the concept of free miles... I have now expanded on that. I expected an average, including stops of 10 mph. This is my baseline. If I go over that without having to pedal, its called free miles... doesn't have to be down hills, can be wind assisted. However I was going so fast today that I decided if I hit 20mph whilst not pedaling it counts as double free miles.... yeah yeah I know I sound like I've lost it lol, but it helps to pass the time.

I freewheeled into Tulsa in record time, having done just around 95 ish miles. Found the Super 8, got a discount (again) and settled down to catch up with everyone. The wifi didn't work... panic stations. I was ready to up and leave but fortunately they sorted it out but it made me slightly sad on one hand and lucky on the other... let me explain...

I like to think of myself as the kind of person who could up sticks and live in a wild place with little of no connection to the outer world... today I realised I probably couldn't and that made me slightly sad, but better than that it made me feel lucky and that is because I have such wonderful family and friends, that on this short trip, it is without question the highlight of my day, shower and bed notwithstanding, to sit and catch up with everyone by facebook and email and I feel lucky because of that.

So on that note... go outside, take a deep breath of fresh air and feel the peace that enveloped me today, then tell someone close to you about it and you will come close to feeling how I do now.

As always Love Hope and Strength to all. Roll on Oklahoma city tomorrow!

Reading this back, I feel i was probably caught up in the journey. It is not just here that I have had perfect moments whilst out cycling. Often they come unexpectedly. Perhaps when you round a bend in the road and catch sight of the hills - like I often do when in Brecon. Or once, not far from where I live, on a quiet country lane, where I encountered some horses quietly grazing in a field. Sometimes I think there would be more perfect moments if the 'rush of life' was not always with us.

It just requires someone to stop and look around them and take in everything quietly..

After over 2 weeks back that is what I miss most - the feeling of space and of freedom, because even though I was constrained by a route and a time limit, these were constraints that I had personally chosen to live by. And the freedom extended beyond where to go, when to stop, what to eat and other activities of daily life on the road. On a bike trip, by myself, the freedom of the road gradually translates to freedom of thought until different thoughts, feelings and memories flow through the mind without a pause in which to dwell upon them. Meditation on the move..

Chapter 16 - Day 9: I am unsafe...

Firstly, thank you to Lynn who took me out in Tulsa last night. It was nice to see some local life, even if I am now painfully aware that I am surrounded by people carrying guns... very weird thought if you live in the UK.

So having got up this morning, once again determined to get an early start, when as you might have seen, I saw the flat back tyre. I knew that I had a very long day ahead and probably a bit tired from not being in bed by 9pm as I am accustomed to doing, and this felt like a bad omen for the day.

I rolled up my sleeves and with hands that don't work as well as they did last week, managed to change the tube, get the wheel back on, reattach the panniers, have breakfast and set off by half 8, which isn't bad. It didn't feel like that though. I was in a foul temper.

Now bad moods are why its a good thing to be travelling alone. If you want to be in a bad mood, you can be, cos the only person you can piss off is yourself. Sometimes you want to be in a bad mood and having someone else there trying to cheer you up, can sometimes make it worse. So temporarily happy with my bad mood, I set off. Quickly my bad mood about the start of the day evaporated and changed to a bad mood with myself for letting a puncture put me in a bad mood... still with me?

Basically it upset me that I had let this get to me. In fact I have been lucky not to have a puncture up till now. The bad mood continued and as a result I was certain that I wouldn't get my rest day, because I thought that I would struggle to get anywhere today, given the late start. The thought of no rest day made my bad mood worse... not even my music was pulling me out of it . Basically my bad mood was further feeding my bad mood and I needed to break the cycle. I glanced down at my bands that I wear constantly (except at work-bare below elbows rule) and got to thinking what they mean to me.

This is what I came up with...
They summarise how I have been able to get through this trip so far

Love - I have such supportive friends and family and friends who are like family that it gives me Hope that I can achieve this challenge that I have set out to do, both of these in turn give me the strength to keep the pedals turning day by day.
Sorry if it all sounds a bit OTT but this is how my thought processes were working at the time.
Once I had thought that through, the music began to filter through...
At this point my decision making was swinging between," just do 60 or so miles today and another short day tomorrow" and "go for it, get it done today and reap the benefit tomorrow". I couldn't make my mind up as to how determined I was going to be. Meanwhile I was making my way through Tulsa and doing a bit of the tourist thing, half convinced that it was going to be a short day.

At some point I started to put the power down, my legs felt good, even if the rest of my body was breaking down. I desperately need a rest day, just to let my hands recover, if nothing else. I also quite needed to visit a pharmacy and a bike shop, to give my bike the once over before the next leg. I also wanted to see the memorial at the least. All this was going through my mind as I pushed harder on the pedals. There were no free miles today and it was like being back in Missouri with the ups and downs

So with my hands on the drops and head into the wind, i was pushing along between 15 and 20 mph, with uphill between 12 and 14mph. This is pretty fast on a loaded bike.

As the day wore on, thoughts of stopping short of Oklahoma city started to fade.

I said, if I am at this point by 4pm, I will have enough light to make it. I made sure I stopped every hour to snack and drink, but kept the stops short.

The point that i had a decision to make came... and it was only 3pm. I was an hour earlier than

I thought I would be.

The negative had turned into positive and a challenge to myself to get to the city. I continued to push, knowing that I had fought every mile to get a rest day and it would therefore be much sweeter.

As i neared the city, I started to relax and look around. I hadn't taken much notice of the sights up to this point and ironically the scenery seemed to improve, the closer I got to the city. At one point a searing pain went through my left thigh and I worried I had torn something so tried to tone down the pushing. Thankfully the pain subsided and I was able to continue at speed.

Oklahoma city is such that a sign announces the city limits 20 miles out. This makes the last 20miles like you are there but not.

So at half 6 pm, having cycled 115 miles, I got to where i had been planning to spend the night, asked for a discount, got one and sunk gratefully into a very nice room.

So maybe my puncture this morning was not as some (kindly) suggested a sign that I needed to take it easy, or take the bus (Fiona), but rather having risen to the challenge, a sign that I can have more hope that I will make it. Today has given me more strength of mind

I'm very happy that I get my rest day tomorrow. I feel slightly broken and therefore I still declare myself unsafe.... just with a touch of satisfaction!

Matter of fact, I am still annoyed with myself for getting annoyed. Surely that was one of the reasons I took on this bike ride - to meet obstacles head on and solve or overcome them.

In fact there were very few major hurdles that I encountered (apart from headwinds). My bike held up well with no major breakdowns, no one threatened my life (without a car that is) and only 4 punctures through the whole trip could easily be considered lucky.

The main obstacle, as so often in life, was the major games my brain was playing with itself, under the heading - 'You can't make it in time'. As with most things, the power of the mind is greater than anything and if you can find ways to turn it to your advantage, the rest should be a breeze!

Chapter 17 - Rest Day: Where were you hiding when the storm broke...

So I'm probably going to confuse after calling this day 10 at breakfast... but decided to call it rest day and tomorrow day 10 as coincides with my mapping.

Nice hotel last night and woke early to Skype home...

Got shit together slowly then set foot out the door.

Rain pouring and I mean pouring down, rivers and lakes forming on the roads but I had a mission today... get to the other side of the city ready for tomorrow, get my bike looked at and visit a pharmacy... reasons discussed later.

So I got pretty wet and went pretty slowly and eventually got to a days inn, which is as far from the best western as chalk from cheese and looks something like the motel in No Country for Old Men.

Doesn't really matter tho... the heater is on full blast, drying my only pair of shorts so I can get wet again when I pop out to get food.

So whilst I am waiting for them to dry, I have CNN on. Its full of the government shutdown and the Obamacare website which doesn't work properly.... a healthcare website not work... really... after spending lots of money on it? Seems it isn't just the NHS then!

The other funny thing that struck me when I watch tv is any health product advert has an almost complete listing of side effects and contact your doctor ifs....during the advert. Its like, buy (insert product name) it may cause chest pain, breathlessness, you could even die, make sure you tell your doc if u suffer with any itching, redness, allergic reaction,... but its really good and may help weight loss. Stop Taking it if you feel dizzy or nauseous.. but do please buy it! And if your insurance doesn't cover it astra zenecca may be able to help you...

Well it made me chuckle...

So my original aim was to go and visit the memorial, but I quickly decided that although it would be a shame not to see it, it was just too wet for me to use up energy fighting my way downtown and then back up again and the energy might well be needed tomorrow, especially if its like this!

On the way I found a bike store, and made an important purchase that will hopefully save me from severe saddle soreness. Somewhat a taboo subject between cyclists and non cyclists.. you have to understand that preventing things getting bad is high priority as that will be one of the few things that could bring all this to an abrupt halt... I cant cycle standing up all the way..

So how do u prevent I hear you ask... well, a good thin saddle (less contact points =less areas of chafing), no underwear under the bike shorts (less seams always a good thing) and chamois cream! Hence my pharmaceutical and bike shop visits. I also bought a white marker which I'm hoping will work on my panniers so I can scrawl a message or two on them.

There seems to be a decent Mexican restaurant outside and will stock up on provisions for tomorrow. I might try and repack the panniers to see if I can do it in a better way to leave more room for souvenirs... I mean provisions.

So keep your fingers crossed that the weather is better tomorrow. I'm still feeling good after yesterdays ride so will take it easy whilst I can.

LHS X

An update on the chafing issue - which surprisingly appeared to be a 'hot topic'. I fully recommend the brand 'Butt'r. After 4 weeks I could still sit on the bike, without too much discomfort and got no... I repeat, no saddle sores. Result!!!!

There are many things that I found fairly strange in the USA... here is a short list:

1. *Drive through ATM machines*
2. *Drive through Laundrettes*
3. *The fact that you can walk in a gun shop and have a firearm in 10 minutes (complete with live ammunition)*
4. *Quarters - until I realise that you need them for the laundrette*
5. *Tipping - a difficult concept for us Brits.*
6. *Serving sizes - Have you seen the large version of a MacDonald's drink.. or the small for that matter?*

7. *Cycling on a motorway - though I was very grateful to be able to do this.*
8. *No one walks, anywhere, period.*
9. *Drive through Pharmacy*
10. *American football - sorry, I just don't get it!*

Chapter 18 - Rest day and Day 10: Fight back...

In contrast to my previous days blogs, I am going to start this days blog from the night before...

As usual I was catching up with messages from friends and family when I received an email. A friend of mine has just been told of a cancer diagnosis. Obviously this upset me a huge amount, especially as this person is one of the truly, genuinely good people of this world, but I am sharing this to put all this adventure into some kind of context.

Whatever difficulty or challenge I face on this journey will never come close to the challenges faced by people battling illness. And it highlights the importance of the work done by Love Hope Strength foundation and Delete Blood Cancer both in the UK, USA and spreading round the world, thanks to the work of people like Mike and Jules Peters, James Chippendale and everyone connected with these charities in the fight.

So before I continue the blog for day 10 - my friend - today I cycle with you in mind... and in the words of MP, Fight back fight back fight back with all that you are!

Day 10 began with an unfortunate glance at the weather update... storms passing over head, flooding in Texas, winds gusting up to 40mph...remind me never to do that again. Its much easier to face the weather as it hits you than dread it coming, but having seen that I was eager to get a good start, just in case things turned really bad.

Of course then everything took longer to do, and I didn't get my foot on the pedal until half 7am and faced westwards out of the city. After the, by now infamous, Highway 100 out of St. Louis I faced the expressway with some trepidation, but needn't have worried. All the cars and trucks were courteous, giving way and giving room and soon I was out on the old Route 66 road, content... well sort of.

Whether it was the rest day or something else, I didn't have the zip I did... ok I had a fairly horrendous head/sidewind to deal with, but it wasn't raining. (Grateful for small mercies me). It was however bloody cold with just shorts and although I had tried, my shoes were not fully dry, meaning neither were my feet, and therefore they were blocks of ice! I was very grateful for my wind/waterproof which did a good job in keeping my core temp above freezing... but the legs were stiff and my foot hurt!

Woe is me right... well actually despite all this and the snail pace I was doing, I was enjoying myself. Once onto the 66 road, I was pretty much by myself, in the middle of just about nowhere, which is my favourite place in the world and the scenery reminded me of the ridgeway... yes hills again but even these were ok, I just trundled up and down setting a steady tempo.

This equilibrium was disturbed slightly about 40 miles in, when I realised the problem of drinking too much on a rest day.. you don't use up the water and now I desperately needed to find a bush...but trying to find a bush on this road was next to impossible and although it had been pretty deserted, every time I thought id found a suitable point to stop a car appeared on the horizon... this went on for at least 10 miles and although the situation was becoming more desperate, I could see the funny side. On one hand, I was too isolated cos no gas station appeared, on the other hand, I wasn't isolated enough cos the cars kept appearing..

Anyway eventually I chanced it, hopped behind some kind of barn and emerged in a short while feeling much better, got on my bike, pedaled 5 mins down the road..... and a gas station appeared!

The road continued ever westwards... one highlight was getting stopped by some road workers and the surprise on their faces when I told them I had come from Chicago 11 days ago and was going to LA, priceless. I have also started to graffiti my panniers, currently LA or bust and some hash marks to count off the days along with the words that keep me going, Love, Hope and Strength! I also got to see a large bird of prey up pretty close and this time it wasn't dead!

The wind remained strong throughout the day but I couldn't shake off the feeling that I was trying to outrun the storm, heading for bluer skies all the time and eventually the sun did break through a little, enough to warm my bones and feet up!

One feature of the landscape that had been ever present since the city, and should have given me a clue as to what kind of day to expect, were the wind-farms, in the hundreds. I did think this was good to see as we hear a lot of negativity about the gas guzzling America, but here was proof, that in some areas at least, alternative sources of energy are being embraced and they do look kinda majestic in the fields that I don't think they detract from the scenery at all.

Once again, I found myself going up hill and down dale alongside the flat interstate. The road itself wasn't in too bad a condition but it was a relief occasionally to hit a wide smooth duel carriageway.

In regards to injuries, my foot has been playing up today, not just when I stand but also whilst cycling. It might have something to do with the cold today, or maybe just because I've cycled over 900 miles on it. My hands still remain weak and weird feeling but I can live with that. My arse is hurting less today, so I guess the day off did some good.

So wearily I crawled up yet another hill to arrive at my destination for today, a small town called Clinton. I was originally going to stop 15 miles further down the road, but there was no where to stay there, according to google maps, so it was a choice between Clinton or Canute, another 20 miles down the road and frankly I'd had enough fresh air today.

The motel I'm in is possibly the wrong side of town (lots of sirens) and is less salubrious than some I've stayed in, but its cheap, they gave me a discount, it has a heater and a bed and most importantly, wifi!

I have noticed that all motels here below a certain price range, have the same floral patterned bedspread and curtains!

So its felt like a long day, but I have had plenty of peace and solitude along the road and have rather enjoyed it today... fingers crossed again for me that the weather holds, it seemed to do the trick today.

So now for a nice hot shower and then settle down to a book and another Hershey bar!

Onwards and westwards to Texas.....

I look back at this post and once again sadness has enveloped me for my friend. We started our journey's at roughly the same time, but whilst mine is done, my friends's has only just begun.

It is once again a reminder of how important the work of LHS (Love Hope Strength foundation) is, how lucky I am to be in good health and how precious life is. I know my friend will be strong and fight back with a smile as always and have plenty of friends, myself included, to share the journey and support in any way possible.

Chapter 19 - Day 11: There are no frontiers....

The tone of todays blog has changed in my head throughout today... This morning did not start well. Once again, I struggled to get up (what? You aren't surprised) and by the time I went off to breakfast it was gone 7am, only to find the door to the lobby locked so no breakfast. So I put on my helmet and headed off before the sun had risen.

Actually this was great because I was treated to a beautiful sunrise and the scenery had somehow changed overnight. No longer the Oklahoma trees but red earth and hillocks with scrub bushes, like what I thought the midwest was going to be.

My good mood dissipated mainly because of the state of the roads here. At first glance you would think they were fine, but the composition of the tarmac made it feel as though I was pedaling through treacle.

I kept looking at my wheels to check for punctures or brakes rubbing or something to explain why I was crawling along. Nope nuthin like that to blame it on. It quickly became clear to me that my head and my legs weren't playing the game today.

Matt D kindly put a piece up on my wall about how when you ride, it creates a void in your head for thoughts to come and go... this is true, but also for the negative ones, which are much harder to remove. So my thoughts turned to the days ahead.... big mistake! The enormity of what I still had to do became almost overwhelming, particularly as I hadn't yet reached the point I had originally intended to reach yesterday. If I was 15 miles behind today, what would tomorrow be. Could I possibly catch up the miles lost and so on. The pressure of a late start added to these thoughts. Now normally I would come up with some phrase or saying to break up the pattern but today these thoughts stuck in my head for a while. I was crawling along at 10 to 12mph on the flat and the wind and the cold were adding to a general lack of oomph.

It took all the willpower I had not to stop at the first motel I saw, crawl into bed with the covers over my head. I was this close to stopping and taking another rest day... what stopped me, well the thought that I may need this day more in the next 2 weeks than I needed it now. Sure things felt crap but they could be worse and who knows what challenges might lie up the road.

So I plodded on until I came to Elk City, the first waypoint for todays ride. Once there , I kinda missed my turning and found myself on a smooth, wide hard shoulder.... the interstate... oh well ... I could always pretend not to know it was illegal, play the stoopid foreigner card if stopped. I loved it... 16mph with little difficulty, flying along, what a difference a good road surface makes. So in this manner I shot along to the next junction, where with regret, I once again joined the frontage road.

For the next few miles of bumpy drudgery I found myself contemplating why I put myself through these things. I love my life back home and am not running away from anything, I am more running towards something I think. ! Many years ago I was in a car accident, we got hit by a lorry on the M25, and although we were physically unhurt, I struggled with the thought that I had dodged the proverbial bullet. It was because of this that the invincibility you feel when you are young was suddenly and brutally replaced with the fear of dying- sorry cheery subject I know. Since then I have always been chasing life, because I realised how precious and short it can be and how quickly it could have gone that day. So I try to pack as much into my life, experience as many things as possible, chase my dreams, because I believe that this is the only shot you get at it.

The ironic thing so far on this trip, whilst I have seen and experienced huge amounts, it has only made me think more about everything and everyone I appreciate back home... I have always expected this though and wear always a pendant with the words, 'the life you seek does not exist' on it, a lyric from a Mike Peters song (of course) which reminds me that however far away I go, all the best things I have in life... my family, friends, work... will all be waiting for me when I get home.
So back to why do all this then.... because I also believe that part of life is testing yourself, making yourself do things that appear too hard, because then you can take those lessons back with you to your real life and use them to enhance the person you are... does that make sense?

Anyway all these thoughts invaded my mind and provided some distraction from the leg aching task of the day.
Now having missed the Oklahoma memorial I was determined to see Texola, the deserted town on the border. I was on my last legs, 7 miles to go, pedaling squares, knackered.... and then Oklahoma decided to say goodbye, by

raining on me.... cold tired and now wet, I was about ready to pitch my tent at the roadside when I saw a sign........

Not from God, but for a cafe... wearily I pulled up with the full knowledge that if I stopped I wouldn't get to Mclean today. I went in and found a beautifully decorated tea room/art gallery. I was asked in a good southern drawl if I wanted anything and soon I was sitting, coffee and cake in hand, chatting to the owner of Tumbleweeds which is both the first and last stop in Oklahoma.

It was fascinating how this lady had been drawn to an old building and turned it into this place, full of art, painted wonderfully by herself and providing a weary traveller with a place to stop. Before I knew it an hour had gone but funnily enough the panic of not making Mclean had gone, replaced by the joy of sharing stories and coffee. This stop reminded me that (although I have to get to LA in time for the gig and flight home, its also about how I get there and the people I meet along the way that make it a journey.

So because of the stop, I set off with renewed fervor... and gave an inner whoop of joy when I crossed the border... ok so it wasn't an inner one, but no one heard (I hope). Texas seemed to recognise my change of mood and welcomed me with sunshine and scenery that some might call boring, but I thought was the picture of perfection...

Cattle lazily grazing in fields of scrub green, which stretched for miles in every direction.... this is how I'd imagined it and it was perfect. The sun lit up the white wisps of clouds as the (now) gentle breeze sent them scudding along. I even saw my first real cowboy, hat and pickup truck, locking in his cattle on the ranch for the night.

The last 10 miles to Shamrock were pure bliss, not because I was flying along, though the road was better, but because I had been re shown the beauty of my surroundings and nothing could spoil that!

Shamrock provided me with the blarney inn and a steakhouse...

That will do...

Texas is currently my favourite state, lets hope that lasts!

The interesting thing is that I don't remember the hardships of this day. I remember more the kindness and hospitality shown to me by the owner of the cafe.

I also remember the joy and relief on entering Texas - in fact considering my new-found habit of crying at every emotional moment, it's a wonder I wasn't in floods of tears here too. Each border crossing was a small step in achieving a difficult task, a moment of momentous import within the whole. Difficult to describe but easy to feel at the time - echoes of which are still resounding in me as I write this. And although the journey as a whole still hasn't sunk in properly (see Chapter 36) moments like this have settled within me.

Chapter 20 - Day 12: Dream aloud...

So I woke up bright and early, feeling good mentally, a bit knackered physically, but what else to expect..

No breakfast again at the Blarney Inn, so I hot footed it up the road to have my first, and I hope last Macdonalds breakfast.

Having paid attention to the great Chris among others, I went and stocked up on food for the day, probably overdosed on bananas, then set off. Now because I was certain that interstate riding is legal in good ole texas, the first thing I did was hop on it. Smooth roads, not much traffic, sun just coming up to reveal endless fields of dry scrub grass, with cattle quietly grazing... this is what I had dreamed of when I set off, a land unlike the one I was born in, something unique. It was completely mesmerising. A few miles in I hopped off the I40 and stopped for 5 mins to take photos of the stunning landscape... behind me a golf cart came chugging up, pulled up alongside and an older gentleman enquired what I was doing... we chatted for a good 15 mins, he told me about his paper round of 5 papers and I told him about my ride and the charity. It was a lovely start to the day and I felt pretty carefree.

Although it was cold, the morning held the promise of warm sunshine and no wind, and the blue sky stretched endlessly. I wish u could all be here to see it! I cant describe it that well I'm afraid and the pics will never do it justice!

So back on the interstate I went until I came to the barbed wire and Route 66 museum in Mclean, which had some cool stuff but just didn't have time to look around, maybe next time! Unfortunately I came out with some more souvenirs, must must stop doing that!

After Mclean there were miles and miles of interstate and nothing else, which was great. There wasn't much traffic, more in Reading on a Sunday, so it wasn't stressful and I got to enjoy the scenery. I climbed up gradually until I hit what's called the panhandle, which was flat and smooth and if you are a cyclist, to die for!

I was making great time and entertained pushing on to do 120 odd miles, whilst conditions were good- but first lunch stop

The Dairy Queen, unhealthy, horrible, but my only choice.. so I sat in there, gulped down a burger and then went back out to my bike... something was wrong... yup you guessed it, another puncture. So off came the panniers, off came the back wheel again and half an hour later, it was all fixed, the brakes were out of whack though and by the time I'd sorted them, an hour had gone the way of the wind.

So still feeling ok, I set off again, aiming for Amarillo and the halfway point of this journey. I was still hopeful that if the wind remained low, I could push on past Amarillo.

As I neared the city though, traffic and junctions became more numerous. The problem with junctions is I had to slow right down, make sure nothing was turning off the interstate and then hop across the exit lane. With that and the traffic, I decided it would be wise to get off and run along the frontage road. Problem with that was where two interstates crossed over the frontage road ran out, forcing me to go in towards the city, which took loads of time.

Due to the lost hour and this detour away from the interstate, it was getting late and the hopes of pushing on were waning. I decided to get as far through Amarillo as possible before calling it a day,

This found me in a lovely, if slightly expensive room with time to do laundry (yes again, remember I only have 2 of everything) and do my nightly catch up with folks from home. Pizza (Chris S. take note) ordered to deliver and counting the cost of the day, in a non monetary sense. The next few days are going to hurt big time. Because of the lack of places to stop, tomorrow I have to get to Tucumcari, 107 miles away, but then there is a whopping 134 miles to the next place, this would then leave me 30 to 40 miles to do on my rest day to get me into Albuquerque! Hmmmm. Well I will certainly give it a good go. It will be on the interstate and hopefully the weather will hold. However there is a distinct possibility that my tent will be put to good use, the day after tomorrow.

So another whoop of joy at getting to the halfway point, a moment of caution as to what the next few days will bring but above all continuing to dream aloud!

I have never liked cycling through cities, if you haven't guessed I'm more of a country and wide-open space kinda person. But looking back over the journey as a whole, Amarillo wasn't that bad to cycle through. The traffic was better than St.Louis and L.A and the frontage road was decent enough.

I laugh now at me thinking that I had reached the half-way point but at least I went to sleep on that thought and didn't discover until the next day that i was actually a fair few miles away from it!

Chapter 21 - Day 13: Lead me through the darkness...

Attempt number 2 at posting this....

So I set off in the dark... don't worry I had lights.. and ironically felt safer on the interstate going out of Amarillo, due to the headlights of the cars and trucks. I quickly realised that I needed my head torch in order to avoid the inevitable debris on the hard shoulder.

Did I mention that it was cold, close to freezing cold, but for the first few miles I didn't notice as I was entranced by the way the sun rose, gradually lighting up my world, I.e the tarmac, until I no longer needed my light to see my way.

After the sun rose, it got colder - weird huh. The wind grew stronger and it got colder as I got further away from Amarillo, meaning that I had to stop every 30 mins to stamp some feeling back into my feet. I couldn't stop for long as not only did the rest of me get colder as my feet warmed up, but I was also painfully aware that I had to make the miles today or risk jeopardising plan b and having to think up a plan c.

I was also made aware of the fact, via a billboard, that I hadn't reached halfway yesterday, signs for the halfway cafe showed a distance of around 25 miles still to go. This made me determined not to stop properly until I got there and it was this that drove me onwards, against the freezing headwind, albeit at a crawling pace. I found myself hating it yet at the same time enjoying it and was muttering incentives/expletives at myself to keep me going! I did stop for 5 mins to stuff down a cookie dough protein bar, which is one of the worst things I have ever tasted. It did the trick however and 3 hours after I had set off, I crawled into the cafe, to be greeted with a hot cup of coffee before I had even sat down.

The cafe had a gift shop, where I managed to avoid buying anything for once and I spent time there taking photos, signing the visitor book and catching up with facebook. A special mention must go to Dave S. here who wished for a tailwind for me and when I finally emerged from the cafe, the wind had changed direction... it was still freezing cold tho, 3 degrees not including the wind chill factor.

Whilst in the cafe, I chatted to a lovely couple about the ride and the charity and nodded to a few bikers, with whom I shared an understanding about the elements on the road. It is talking to people like this that make this about the journey, not just the destination.

So once again I set off, and with the wind behind me, I managed a good pace.

The Texas panhandle is at quite a height and when I reached the point where the road descends off the plateau, the view that greeted me, beautiful, desolate and vast made me fairly emotional. Whether it was the fact that I had battled hard to get here, or maybe it was the thought this morning that I wouldn't get this far today, or just the sight of such a spectacular landscape, but as I prepared to descend, tears sprang to my eyes.

Now descending in itself isn't easy at speed, but add in a fully loaded bike, a side/tailwind and dodging road debris, it made for an adrenaline fuelled 15 mins. At that point, one of the bikers that I had nodded to, sped past, beeping his horn, his fist lifted in a triumphant salute of solidarity on the road, this and the scenery were my reward for the hours of toil I had endured... I felt on top of the world....

As I descended it got slightly warmer, it was still cold, but warmer nonetheless. With the greater speed lifted the worry about making the miles and I was able to get my head up and enjoy the views.

I stopped at the motor museum and although I don't particularly have an interest in cars, I was viewing the history of Route 66 that I am now feeling connected with.. that and a nice hot cup of coffee, set me up for the next leg of the day.

I continued along the road and as I crossed the border into New Mexico I let out another inner whoop of joy to have reached my 5th state in 13 days. New Mexico greeted me with sunshine and with the pressure of making the miles planned lifted for the day, I was able to relax and enjoy the views. Although I was on the interstate there were stretches where I was alone and I found the inner peace that comes to me when I am surrounded by nature and breathing fresh air. The view remained breathtaking with mountains rising up in the distance and vast areas of scrubland stretching out in front of my wheels.

I'm not sure I mentioned in my blog yesterday about my first snake sighting (live), not a rattler but still. It was lucky to remain alive, I just managed a last minute dodging maneuver as it slithered into the scrub. With this in mind, I kept my eyes firmly on the road ahead and to the side in the hope of seeing a rattlesnake, whilst still dodging debris, including 2 areas of nails strewn across the shoulder. Unfortunately did not see one, but if I do, rest assured I will get my camera out!

The next stop was at a place that my actual mother as well as my work mothers would have frowned upon me visiting, a truckers rest stop, but it was here that I met Jesse, a cancer fighter, who was very interested in the ride and the charity and kindly offered to spread the word on facebook, as well as offering advice on what to do in electrical storms and tornados. He might also be in LA for the end of ride gig and it would be pretty cool to see him there. It is meeting people like Jesse that make my day complete and I hope I meet many more people like him on this journey. So thank you to him...

The last 30 miles or so to Tucumcari were more of the same special scenery and I really enjoyed it, the legs felt good, even on the hills and the sun warmed my bones up. When I reached the town, I turned off the interstate and felt so good I didn't stop at the first motel I saw! Instead I leisurely made my way along the main road, taking in the old buildings and feeling at peace with the world.

I stopped at one motel, got settled in, only to find the wifi didn't work. Now despite being British, I complained, packed up, got my money back and strolled across the road to another motel.

Now just a warning, tomorrow I have a huge day, 134 miles to cover, so will be setting off early and finishing late, but I may not be able to blog. SPOT will tell you that I am safe, but I need to cover the miles in order to have a short 30 ish miles into Albuquerque for my rest day the day after tomorrow.

So I have been led through the darkness, through the tears (tho not bitter) and guided to hope...
LHS as always

The couple in the cafe deserve another mention because not only did Faith follow my blog from that day on, she gave me advance warning about the road ahead and helpful hints and tips on which route to take. Her information was invaluable and often steered me on a better course. I still find such kindness overwhelming - the fact that they were interested enough in my little journey still amazes me and I want to thank them again for helping to make this journey the special experience it was.

Chapter 22 - Day 14: Hardland, ripped and torn apart...

They say a picture speaks a thousand words but today I'm not sure any of the 4 pics I took would even come close to telling the tale...

I think I set myself up for failure today... 134 miles ambitious even with all conditions perfect...

I'd got up reasonably early but was kicking myself that I didn't set off before the sun came up. Breakfast was not offered where I was staying so off I went, but found nowhere open between the motel and the freeway... mistake number 1. I did eat some more of the god-awful cookie dough and some other bits and pieces left from yesterday so I wasn't without sustenance.

I had had it on good authority that there was a big hill on the way out from Tucumcari and as I hit it, before my legs had stopped the screaming, I thought that this wasn't the best way to start the day,

Did I also mention that it is still pretty cold here...once again my feet turned to ice blocks and although (Dunne) I have been colder it wasn't great to start the day with numb toes.

The morning sky was full of the promise of a beautiful day... the sun was shining over the hills and some warmth hit the ground. The sky was sooo blue, without a single wisp of cloud and for short while all was well.

The initial hill climb was ok, long but not too steep and after Chris's welsh training camp, I span up it with a reasonably good pace, got to the top and took a photo smiling brightly... the shadows were definitely laughing at my joy tho, because once at the top, the wind grabbed hold of me with a vengeance, head/side wind once again, slowing my progress to a crawl, almost knocking me off my bike at times with a strong gust. It took a good amount of energy to keep the bike going straight, never mind up and straight.

And up is where the road was going... never really steep but long long drags ever upwards (no one mentioned the 2nd to 5th climbs). Downhill sections provided no respite because even pedaling I was scarcely reaching forward momentum speed.

All the while time ticked rapidly onwards until 3 hours had gone and I hadn't made any headway. On one of the good days I would have been at Santa Rosa by this time so with every second that ticked by, the goal of the day seemed more and more doomed to fail... I say fail cos that how it seems, I set my mind to do stuff and then go do it, but time was not on my side and darkness would hit and if things continued in this way, I would be looking at 2 to 3 hours cycling in the dark. I wouldn't have minded too much, but remain ever conscious of the promises I have made to many people to stay safe.

What other options do I have... this was primarily what I was debating in my head as I continued the struggle towards Santa Rosa. I also had a slight panic moment when I thought my tab had died and my connection to everyone gone... it was only momentary but did stress me out somewhat!

One thing which managed to raise a smile were the advertising hoardings. Since leaving Tucumcari, i had been searching for a place to stop and fill up on food and up till that point had drawn a blank... the advertising hoardings were promising me 24 hour breakfast and all the food I could ever want... only in 100 miles :) ahh no problem then! Even the ones advertised as 20 minutes away would be a good couple of hours for me and although it made me smile, it showed how small the world has become and how little room for adventure when 100 miles away is worth advertising! The hoardings are also the bane of my existence, given that Its sometimes hard enough to keep going without the promise of bed, wifi and shower at every junction! I eventually found a small gas station and stocked up, including Hershey's cookies and cream which I am just about to break open. (well everyone keeps telling me I need calories). Food found and eaten, but I didn't find it any easier, contrary to the popular belief that me with food =happy me... it was all headwind dependent today, I can guarantee you.

Given the large amount of effort being expended to stay on the straight and narrow and not be blown into the path of an oncoming truck, I didn't take many pics, but the scenery remained spectacular, perhaps even more so than yesterday, with the hills appearing in the middle of the grassland and stretching out to the horizon - and I was appreciating it - somewhere in the recesses of my brain, I have stored the views from the tops of the climbs, the colour of the red earth and the way it contrasted with the golden scrub grass and the bright blue sky. Still haven't seen any rattlers but I have seen where they would have been, had I time to go and look, and I was tempted :)

I also got offered a lift by an actual cowboy, hat and all!

All this is just delaying explaining my decision to stop early to you and justifying it to myself. I have tried to explain how vicious the wind was today, but a risk I'm taking is that it would be no better tomorrow and which case so be it.. but mainly my exertions from climbing hills and battling the wind has left me mentally and physically exhausted today and I have one eye on the overall goal of this game, to get to the end, yes in time for the gig, but also to get there in one piece. This led me to thinking about the different phases this journey has and what that means to me...

Phase 1 - The beginning.. full of excitement, hope and In good physical condition. Everything is new and holds interest.

Phase 2 - The middle, the hard slog, the bit where the initial excitement has worn off and you just gotta keep going. Physically everything starting to hurt. Routine set and mastered (hopefully)

Phase 3 - The end of the challenge is within touching distance and fears about not completing wane. Excitement of thoughts of seeing friends and family again. Aches and pains forgotten.

So thats what I reckon the stages of most journeys like this are, and I am firmly in the hard slog of stage 2... but not for long. In a few days i will be entering my 7th state (sorry to Kansas for missing you out on yesterdays blog!) With just the 1 more after that and then phase 3 will begin... and hopefully I will be smiling all the way to the pier.

So I argued with myself for 10 miles.. and I won! Part of me is pissed off with myself for taking the rest day today (I did do 56 miles today, but still...), the other part of me knows that I was close to 80% done in and it was better to stop before that became 100%, to rest and recharge in order to begin hurtling towards phase 3 (or if it is like today, turning the pedals round one at a time)!
So I threw out my plans (again), rewrote them, and stayed flexible, which I think, when all is said and done, will be the key to getting to the finish.

This Hardland has ripped and torn me apart today, hard dreams have left me scarred
But this is only today....

I can still hear the wind in my ears as I read this blog back to myself. It's very easy in hindsight to say that stopping early on this day was the right thing to do.. but at the time it felt like a huge failure on my part. Kinda like, 'when the going gets tough, the tough just stopped'.

On a better note, I was chuffed to see that Mike Peters had left me a message on my facebook page concerning this day.

Previously the anonymous 'good authority' mentioned in this day's blog he had kindly warned me about the initial hill out of Tucumcari before I left. He left a lovely message of encouragement and apologised for not mentioning the other 2 or 3 hills I had to climb that day (LOL).

Just a good example of the kind of man he is - to take time out of his VERY busy schedule to read my blogs and then boost my spirits with a message - total and utter legend!

Chapter 23 - Day 15 - Trying to make it to the end of the world...

Trying to make it to the end of the world
Trying to make it to the final 3rd
Whenever I fall down you pick me up
Whenever I fall to pieces you put me back together
You keep on telling me
You keep on telling me to believe

The above song struck a chord with me today... after the hell of yesterday, I woke up this morning with a new outlook on life... saw the weather channel -predicting strong westerly winds but knew I had to get today done.

I had a leisurely breakfast.. too leisurely I guess and poked my head outside to be pleasantly surprised... no wind. I got cracking and headed to the interstate and the first 2 miles were glorious. The sun was out, it was warm, a gentle breath of wind, a bit of downhill. Life good again. Turned westwards and was hit by a wall, the same wall that had conquered me yesterday. Only this time, I set my teeth, faced up to the wind and stamped on the pedals, determined to beat this today.

You see, I couldn't change the wind direction and couldn't change the direction of the road, the only thing I could choose to change, was how I reacted to it. I could once again accept that I was going to have a crap day or I could choose to take the wind head on and score a personal victory. And try and enjoy....

Difficult but not impossible... I was grateful it wasn't cold or raining for starters and once again the view was to die for.

The first 5 hours were spent on an almost constant climb, none too severe, just relentless. Upward was the only way, do I turned up the music to try and drown out the howling wind and kept the legs going round. Unfortunately, due to the constant battering, I was going at best 8mph and that was on the short sections of downhill, which I would normally reach speeds of up to 30mph!

If you want to get some idea of the experience you could do one of 2 things: Drive along at 25 mph, lower your window and stick out your hand, palm facing forwards.. that is how much I was being battered. To replicate the effort, go to the gym, get on a bike and put the gears to 14 or 16. Pedal for 1 hour, then multiply that by 12 in your head and that was my day!

I'm not complaining (too much). Every stop I had (one 5 min every hour) I sat up, and took in the views.... once again vast desolation, making me feel very insignificant in the grand scheme of things and although I had cars and lorries passing my left, I was in my own headspace and felt like I was in a bubble of my own, with my thoughts to keep me company

Some of these thoughts were turned to Melanie and her family. Melanie lost her fight a few days ago and is the friend of a friend. Although I never knew her, I feel connected to each and every one of the names on these flags and feel a responsibility to get them to the end of the pier. I had been asked to get a photo of her name in a nice spot and in due course I managed that... the story of the picture comes later but today I rode for Melanie....

So I battled and battled, mile after mile (I am not exaggerating) - I fought tooth and claw, crawling along at best. It didn't matter though, today it was going to take me as long as it took, and although Albuquerque (yes that bloody place again) once again seemed to be slipping out of reach, i continued to hope that conditions would improve. This continued for 50 ish miles, when finally I came to a good place to stop for food. By this time it was 1pm, and although tired of wind, my determination to see this day through hadn't waned in the slightest.

At this stop I met my boost for the day.. a young couple, Austin and Jess (hope I have remembered the names correctly) asked me what I was doing. So we chatted for 15 mins or so about cycling (They wanted to do a bike trip from Utah, where they live), the charity and swopped stories. Once again, this made my day. They were kind enough to give me a can of Monster, gratefully received and we parted, hopefully to stay in touch, maybe even to see them at the gig in LA. (yes gig, not concert...you know who you are)

Having eaten, I had hoped that the next stage would be better, but once again, got greeted by my old friend, headwind... and so it continued. It was around this time that I tried to get the photo of Melanie's name on the flag as the scenery was breathtaking, but the strength of the wind made it impossible, so on I went.

A few miles later, the wind dropped slightly and i thought that this was my chance... I had severe difficulty trying to unclip my cleats on both sides, and had pain shooting up my left (possibly fractured) foot. I could not unclip and in exasperation, said out loud, "cmon, give me a break". I swear I heard laughter shortly before a violent gust put me to a complete standstill, leaving me no where to go but down on my backside... and apparently my finger also cos a chunk of flesh is now missing.
Ironically it made me laugh, as i stood up, I again said out loud, "apparently not then"... fortunately my damaged finger

was the worst of my injuries. However I did manage to get the photo this time...

Onwards and upwards went the road and conditions not improving in the slightest. I had been promised for the last 20 or so miles a place called Clines Corners, a famous Route 66 stop off point and eventually after another few hours of hard graft I got there. It was half 5pm and daylight was running out with 15 or so miles to go. My strategy at this point was to eat now, to save eating later and hope that with the sun disappearing over the horizon, the winds would die down..and they did a bit, which meant that after food, I could up the mph slightly.

Shortly after this I reached the plains marker which indicated that I had climbed to 6500 Feet and ticked another box.

There was still a sting in the tail in the form of another long drag uphill, one that lorries had their hazards on all the way up, but was determined to make it to the top. Eventually I did, and stopped and appreciated the calm and peace of the moment.... The last 12 miles were downhill, facing the setting sun, disappearing over the tops of the distant mountains and silhouette them against the dusk sky and although those mountains carried the promise of pain tomorrow, I felt nothing but sincere joy to be alive and witness to such beauty. This was my reward today.

Because of the drop in windspeed and the gentle downhill gradient, I was making good speed, trying to outrun the dark. I couldn't so the last 5 miles saw my world narrow to a spot of light from my head torch, and occasionally expand, with the car headlights. I went slowly, mainly to avoid debris and a puncture and although far from ideal and slightly nerve wracking, it added to the adventure and achievement of the day.

So I crawled into Moriarty, a town that had been imploring me to stay the night on billboards 100 miles ago. It felt like destiny that I was to be here. Albuquerque was once more out of reach today, and I'm still slightly behind schedule, but today felt like victory, not defeat.

Which is why the song lines rang true, you all have been putting me back together every night with your posts and words of encouragement and you tell me to believe... after today I have a little more belief that I will carry these flags to the end of the world.

A few reflections on this day's blog. Firstly about choice. I realise that I make it sound quite simple to choose how to react to things you are battling against, things that you cannot change, precisely because I believe it is that simple. I think

everyone has the capacity to choose differently from what they would normally do... they just have to make that choice. Even choosing to do nothing is still a choice, not always a good one though.

Even if all power is removed from you in a situation, you can still choose how you deal with that loss of power or control, wether it be with a smile or anger... for example.

On a different note those last 12 miles were amongst the best I had on the journey. It felt good to put aside all doubts and fears (cycling in the dark in a strange country) and just cycle for all I was worth. And the setting sun made me feel as though I was the last person on the planet, so totally was my focus on the road and my surroundings that my sphere of consciousness extended only to the necessary things - leaving things like cars and lorries outside my world view.

Chapter 24 - Day 16: I refuse to break....

Last night I had to phone a friend for a favour.... my shorts have given up before me and lets just say, the only thing keeping me modest is the fact that I am wearing cycle shorts underneath! Thankfully she is kindly going to get me some for when we meet up, so thank you Louize!

This morning when I woke... for some reason I had a huge bout of homesickness. Whether it was reading email and posts from family or friends or just because I had been physically and emotionally depleted yesterday, the fact was that I spent most of the morning thinking about different people at home and wishing they were here to see this place with me.

Anyway, after breakfast, I set off early, determined a) not to finish in the dark b) to catch up the lost miles and c) to get past Albuquerque before lunch... that place will haunt my dreams I swear. The morning was crisp and cold but looked like it was going to be sunny and although I hadn't dared to believe the weather channel, the wind was light to non existent! Bonus... but I wasn't going to take any chances... weather can change in the blink of an eye... so I set off with purpose. The climb out of Moriarty hurt as my legs hadn't warmed up and although gradual, I was steadily gaining a good amount of height.

It at least kept me warm and I had left off my long fingered gloves and waterproof jacket. I got to the top of the climb in a good time and started the descent...

It was long, winding, and dropped down a magnificent mountain pass and I thought that this was reward for getting up there.

My fingers hovered over the brakes as it was pretty steep in places and didn't want to take any chances.

I rounded a bend to find flashing lights so jammed on the brakes and slowly freewheeled past a lorry on its side, which had overturned and then slid along the barrier, so that the cab was in a ditch. This shook me up quite a bit. I have a particular dislike of lorries anyway due to being hit by one in a car on the M25, but this accident was pretty recent and it made me think that if I had been at that spot at the wrong time, I would have had no chance. It reminded me that no matter how careful I am being, shit luck could always happen! I didn't really enjoy the rest of the descent, partly cos of the lorry but also I was bloody cold. I didn't stop to take pics, which was a shame, but just wanted to get the hell outta there, and to a nice warm cafe.

I eventually got to the bottom and pulled off at the first exit, found a Macdonalds and got a hot coffee which made me feel better. I set off pretty quickly as wasn't yet at Albuquerque (which I need to put behind me and then can stop having to spell it).

When I did get to that place, I didn't hear any fanfare as I felt would gave been fitting. I have been trying to get here for three days, and I was sick of the place before I had even seen it.

As it was it had one main street running through it... the 'famous Route 66 Nob hill' but apart from a bike lane and downhill to the centre, had nothing really worth stopping for. Paid in spades for the downhill on the way out but was so pleased to be leaving Albuquerque (last time of spelling that!), that it didn't matter. And once again, the view from the top, as well as the 'you are now leaving' sign made it worth it.

On leaving, the scenery changed. Before there were scrub bushes and grassland but now this became sandy and fewer green shrubs.. more desert like and in the distance and to the sides rose escarpments of red rock, signalling the passage towards Arizona and canyonlands.

The road was up and down from here on in but in contrast to the preceding 2 days, I was getting just reward for the uphill toil, downhill at speeds of 25mph and upwards, where the legs and arse got a bit of a break. Once again I became lost in the view and thoughts of home. As I said in my earlier facebook post, I am enjoying the adventure, but miss family and friends and feel lucky to have that to miss.

It was also at this point that I regret using up the superlatives too early in my descriptions as New Mexico is breathtakingly stunning. Everywhere I looked, there was a mountain in the distance, rising up from the desert like floor to a perfect blue sky. It was at this point that I managed a flag photo, because I felt that this was a place for a fitting tribute to the names on the flags.

I was in good spirits, it felt like the big part of the day was done, yet I still had 70 miles to go for plan A to work. The trouble was that I kept stopping to take photos wanting to imprint this place on my mind, the way I felt it had imprinted on my soul. Some places are like that... if you are lucky maybe more than one... in my case Switzerland and Poland and now New Mexico. All share a ruggedness in their beauty which I could appreciate.

Eventually I reached what I thought was my plan B point, but the time was good so decided to eat, only to discover that it was the next casino/hotel that was my plan B, and actually I was still 25 miles from plan A. Considering I had been motoring on the flat and downhill sections, this was a slight disappointment so I set myself a time limit to be back on the road. I reasoned that barring incident, I could easily do that in 2 hours which would be half 6 arrival. I sought local knowledge as to the gradient of the road. The reply... well theres a big hill in about 4 miles but once that it done you should be fine!

When I set off again, I should have realised that when a car driver says big hill, a cyclist would have added the word very! However I set a good pace up it as it wound round the edge of one of the hills. Then downhill all the way... errr nope. Again a car drivers view very different, but gradually I saw the miles count down on roadsigns. At about 11 miles to go I was hit by a slight headwind and the sun was starting to fall.

I was also battling with 2 things... aside from the usual road debris I was also dodging what initially looked like scorpions but on closer, slower inspection turned out to be massive locusts/crickets. Then whilst trying not to squash them my left eye started stinging... suncream in the eye is not fun and for several miles I went along with one eye shut or blinking furiously to try and clear it. Amusing maybe, but not when you are on your last legs, and lorries are passing close, and the glare from the sun means the road is not easily seen! I was reluctant to stop but did so, cleared my eye and readied myself for the final push... Easier said than done after 103 miles of up and down. So it was more of a crawling pace that saw me into Grants and to the motel 8 that was waiting with beckoning doors.

Once settled in, I had a lovely phone call from work, which made me smile and cut through my weariness so thanks for that guys!

So I am now, for today at least, back on schedule and spending the night where I was supposed to. It was a mammoth day but today I have refused to break and been rewarded but end the day as I began, slightly homesick and feeling lucky!

The 'What if' of this day still scares me slightly. If I had been 10-15 minutes earlier setting off, I would have been crushed against the side of the road by that lorry. It reminds me how sometimes life hangs in the balance of coincidence and chance and fuels my passion for living life for the 'here and now'.

The homesickness never really abated after that day. It was kept at bay by the frequent contact I had with home, family and friends and coming home was as good as the journey itself.

Chapter 25 - Day 17: Spiritual regeneration every single time we breathe...

Well last night and this morning saw me mending stuff! Yesterday, I forgot to mention in my blog that I had been having severe trouble unclipping my feet from the pedals. For the uninitiated basically I have metal bits on the bottom of my shoes that click into the pedals and to unclip, before you get to a standstill preferably, you have to twist your foot.

My left foot hurts severely whenever I do this so I have tried to use my right foot, which is fine until it stops working. Basically throughout the whole of yesterday, both feet took turns to refuse to unclip, no matter how hard I twisted or pulled.... this, as you can imagine is not ideal, especially for unplanned stops, and the risk of ending up on your backside is a very real one. So I spent most of the latter part of the day, cycling with one foot permanently unclipped, which destroys power transfer from your legs to the pedals.... right thats the technical part done... basically they were broke so with advice over facebook from Chris S. and fortunately a spare pair of cleats, I changed them... only by getting on my bike could I assess if that had solved that one!

This morning saw me with needle and thread, trying to sew my shorts back together... hmmm, lets just say my mum's needlework skills did not rub off on me!

So once again, an early breakfast, which saw me chatting to another trucker, only this time he was telling me how dangerous the interstate was and how people do get killed. Well yes, but if I had worried about that too much, I would have never set foot on my bike. Nevertheless, his words were ringing in my ears when I set off.

I was a bit stressed this morning, I took too long to pack up and my planned point of stoppage seemed not to have anywhere to stay, meaning I had to cycle further than planned, fine but I was now late in setting off.. I had asked the receptionist what the road was like... upwards until Gallup, then good from then. I did take this with a pinch of salt though!

So off I went, having first checked unclipping... it worked hooray.... aiming to get to Gallup by middayish, 60 miles away. Naturally the road climbed up out of town but once again, the gradient was ok. I had seen the weather report before I set off and knew temperatures were close to freezing so had my gloves and jacket on already. And boy was it cold... my toes went numb after 10 minutes, even with the climb. I cycled for about half an hour at an easy pace, to acclimatise the legs for the rest of the day, then stopped to take my usual morning picture. The sky was clear, no wind again (what had I done to deserve 2 days in a row) and once at the top of the climb, I reached a plateau of scrub with some rugged outcrops of rock in the distance, which the morning sunshine lit up. The railway was running beside the road and it made me feel as though I had been transported back in time, however briefly, to the day when the railroad had been the main means of travel across this vast country.
In the 60 miles to Gallup, I considered what to write in this blog as it looked as though the day was just going to be an a to b day, with nice scenery but boring to read about... I came up with road debris as a topic... of which I have become quite a connoisseur. Apart from dead animals (and a deer, an owl and a cat can be added to the list now) most of the debris seems to have flown off lorries, wheel rim, bits of tyre, hooks, bungees

and rope, all seem to be flying off at a great rate, which led me to wondering whether I would be unlucky enough to get hit at some point... thinking Massa in F1.

I hopped off the interstate on to the frontage road, and am so glad I did, because I met another crazy fool, I.e another touring cross country cyclist. This was the first one I had met since I started and we swopped road stories for a while. So nice to meet someone else travelling the road and this was one of the incidents that made this day the best one since starting! I told him stories of large crickets and he in turn told me about tarantulas, perhaps slightly surprised by my gleeful reaction.

Shortly after this, as I was dodging debris, I saw movement, swung my bike round it and registered 8 furry legs and an unmistakable, live tarantula. I was so surprised, that I kept going, before thinking that I should have stopped to take a photo. But by the sounds of it, I should see a few more, but this was another piece to add to making up a great day.

The day was not without its difficulties, and this section of hard shoulder was stony, gravelly, bumpy and generally more suited to a mountain bike. It was complete fluke that I didn't get a puncture, and although frustrating to be bumping along next to a smooth bit of road, I decided it was definitely safer to remain where I was, rather than chance the main lane.

I stopped a fair few times to take photos, before reaching Gallup at around 1pm, in time for a cup of coffee and some food at Dennys and a chat with the lad who was serving me about bike trips and his dreams of one day going on a long one.

Gallup itself was quite a large town and I decided to cycle through to see any Route 66 markers, of which there were none, the older part of the town was pleasant enough, but once again, nothing yelled out at me to stop and take a closer look. I was soon on the interstate, rolling westwards again and remember thinking to myself that it felt like I had broken the back of today's ride. Gallup is also home to what seemed like hundreds of prairie dogs, at least that's what I think they were.. and as I passed they dived for the safety of their burrows whilst leaving a head poking out to observe the ongoings!

Once out of Gallup, the scenery changed again. I was surrounded by rocky cliffs, rising up on either side as the road threaded its way round and through and ever upwards.

Even more spectacular as it went on, I lost myself once again to it. This majestic landscape continued as the miles disappeared under my wheels and once again I wish that I could describe the immenseness that dwarfed everything that man had made around it, enough to do it justice, but I cannot find the words.

Then I reached the continental divide, officially the highest point on this road at 7295 feet and the point where I began to feel phase three starting. From now on, the road would inexorably slope down to the pacific ocean. Thats not to say that there wouldn't be any more climbs to overcome, but rather I was now on the homeward straight. I was sooo chuffed, I went and bought a souvenir!

As I span along, the mile markers were counting down to the state border and here I have to give people that do not know me well, insight into me, in order to give more meaning to what follows..... I tend to keep my emotions inside me and deal with them quietly (I think thats a fair assessment of myself)... I don't like outbursts of emotion, it can make me angry with myself. I don't criticise others who do, but its just not me.

So that said, I continued along, counting down to mile 0. As I approached the boarder I had to choke back tears, that were threatening to blind me (not good whilst going downhill at 25 mph). The surroundings, the passing through the continental divide and the approach to my 7th state after over 1500 miles once again overwhelmed me. This was the point where I started to really believe that I might actually make it to the pier and justify the faith that has been shown in me by family and friends.

Just before I reached the state line, my hard shoulder ran out and I ended up going through the lorry weighing station, receiving waves as I did so. Made me laugh.

The Arizona state sign... another way point on this journey that has been filled with them. One more step closer to home....

Once into Arizona, the rocky outcrops and cliffs receded into the distance, leaving a large plain of grassland and scrub bushes. 25 miles to go and my legs were infused with energy as the end of the day approached.

Arizona didn't make things totally easy and there were a few stiff climbs to negotiate on now tiring legs, but with plenty of time until sunset, I wasn't concerned and took my time. I sped past the initial stopping point with the knowledge that by keeping going, I would for the first time this trip, actually be ahead of schedule. The petrified forest is coming tomorrow and with those extra miles done, I can look forward to some extra time to take photos there.

Those last 6 miles hurt.. and I do mean hurt! Over 220 miles in 2 days. Not wholly surprising. Also in the back of my mind was the worry that I hadn't seen an advertising billboard for the motel, unusual by this point. But relief came with three miles to go... wifi, shower and a bed awaited... if they had a room!

They did and I crawled into it, before changing and heading to the restaurant.... ate food, feel sick... have eaten too much today.

Whilst I was eating I was simultaneously reading a book about a woman who dared to dream big, and by big I mean massive. For 5 years she walked around the world in memory of her husband whom she had lost to cancer. Her story and others like it show that anything is possible, for anyone... you just have to let go of the fear in order to live.

So today I begin to believe...

The only thing I have to add to this day's blog was that once again I was mistaken. The Continental Divide is not the highest point - that award goes to the Arizona Divide at 7335 feet, which means I bought a souvenir under false pretences!

Chapter 26 - Day 18: All cards are marked and all fates will collide...

I opened my eyes this morning, looked at my watch and thought, oh shit!

It was 7am and I had overslept. Normally I'm just putting my feet in the pedals at this point and my plans for the day were already going awry!

It is testament to the practice I have had that I had packed up and had breakfast in 45 mins, desperate to be on the road... I was on a tourist mission today and the painted desert and petrified forest were my aim.

Just as I was putting on my helmet, I glanced through the glass windows to the lobby of the motel and caught sight of the clock... it was 6:55. Laughing to myself at not realising that once again I had gained an hour I set my feet on the pedals and set off.

The first thing I had to get past today, was the closed off bridge that led to the westwards I40 and Winslow, my destination for the day, only 91 miles away! I walked tentatively up to the workman and begged to be let across, knowing that if they didn't let me, I would have to go east at least 10 miles in order to cross over. Once again, all worries were fruitless as I was not only let across, but personally escorted, and then wished a safe journey!

So set in my way, I pedalled for the customary half hour... my legs felt reasonable, despite the chill of the morning air, and once again, the breath of the wind was on my back and the sun was shining. I soon warmed up but didn't stop long enough to discard layers as I wanted to cover the 20 miles to the petrified forest and painted desert national park quickly enough to spend some time there. I made really good progress, all the while watching out for another tarantula appearance (for Barney and Sarah k. especially). The scenery started to change quietly, turning from scrub to more desert like red sand with mounds of rock sticking up from the ground. These rocks got bigger and more numerous but still nothing like that of the google pictures. Before I knew it I was at the exit for the national park and swung in... photo opportunities taken at the sign marking the entrance, I then made my way into the visitor centre.

At the centre I took the opportunity to stamp my passport with stamps for both the desert and the forest and got chatting to one of the park wardens about the cycle ride. Displayed were some of the petrified wood chunks, wood that was buried and turned to stone over many millennia and I then discovered that to see the wood in the park I would have to cycle towards the end of the loop, which was 28 miles, and then back again... too much time... but I could cycle to the viewing points a few miles away.. so I did. The painted desert jumps out at you, you go along the road, wondering where it is, go round a bend and stare out over a canyon, the walls of which are layers of colorful rock stretching down and down below you to the valley floor. I will try not to make up any superlatives (shamazing being one I will not use) but instead describe what I saw and leave the rest to your imagination...

The valley floor was a maze of dry rivulets, curving through a pale red sand. These rivulets were surrounded by pale green scrub, creating a patchwork effect.. this stretched out round smaller mounds of red earth and whiter rock to the edge of the canyon, where it met the rock walls. These walls had coloured layers of brown, grey, white and red stone, which stretched up to the point where I was standing. On the far side this contrasted with the golden scrub grass of the plains which was glowing in the early morning sunlight. I just stood and stared for what seemed like hours until I collected myself and started photographing the 180° panorama. Eager to escape the 'crowds' (about 5 people)I got back on my bike and went to the next viewpoint. Here I sat on the wall, listening to the sound of the wind, and watching the crows hover on the thermals, deafened by the silence and overwhelmed by the peace.. no tears (yet)!

I was caught up by the crowds and having got a few photos standing on top of this creation of nature, being conscious of the miles still to cover, tore myself away, and freewheeled back to the visitor centre. On exiting, I was nearly lost to this place, as the park warden mentioned something about hikes down to the floor and a back country camping permit... I almost asked where I could leave my bike!

Head ruled the heart though and I made my way back to the interstate, shaking my head in disbelief of the experience I had just had. Some of the visitors had just driven up in their cars, snapped a few photos from inside and driven off again... what a way to miss out!

Before I left I bought supplies for the day at the gas station and whilst there bumped into Marty, who had unfortunately lost a family member to leukemia recently and donated to the ride... thank you.

My next waypoint was the town of Holbrook, another 20 miles or so away... but once again this flew past, with music and the rock walls to keep me company, not all downhill, but at a good speed nonetheless. I arrived there in time for lunch and stopped once again at Dennys.

Here, probably because of my appearance... torn, dirty shorts, weird tan lines, helmet dented hair... I was asked about where I had come from, what I was doing so took a few minutes to

spread the LHS word. After exiting the restrooms, I discovered a gentleman called Bob, who had clearly waited for me. He had overheard my conversation and wanted to know more. On top of that he also donated to the ride... another kind act to a total stranger. I shook his hand and set off again, through Holbrook to rejoin the interstate. I felt totally carefree, relaxed about making the last 60 miles in time as the conditions were perfect. This meant I stopped frequently to take photos and gaze out at the view. Of course with every stop, I scanned the ground for movement in hope, but it was not to be today.

Marty had warned me that I would be climbing up to 7000 feet, he seemed taken aback that this did not worry me, until I explained that I had already passed 7295 feet at the continental divide. So the road wound gradually upwards, but not in any way that remotely troubled my legs... it was at this point that I was reminded that I was on an interstate when a lorry veered onto the shoulder, but only briefly but it served as a reminder to stay aware.

During the next 30 miles, there were constant billboards inviting me to go and see the worlds largest petrified tree.

I ummed and ahhhed about whether to stop again, but found I couldn't resist, having seen the worlds largest rocking chair and here comes the story in the title to today's blog. I drew up to the tree, took some photos and touched the ancient stone for luck. I then wandered in to the shop. Here I met two more lovely people, Angelena T and Janice B, who seeing that I had arrived by bike, gave me a can of coke and asked about the ride. I was telling the story of Love Hope Strength Foundation and how I became involved, when I stopped and listened. On the radio playing was Keep on Rocking in the free world.... Now for those unfortunate souls who have not been introduced to the music of The Alarm, this song was recorded by Mike Peters, the founder of the charity, and The Alarm in the 80s.... it was part of the Raw Album that my dad had given to me to listen to when I was a teenager... it was the song that had begun this journey.. in so much that it led me eventually back to The Alarm and to Love Hope Strength years later. All fates will collide... it appeared in that moment that they had. I don't believe in signs really, but this is as close as I have ever come to thinking that this journey was somehow meant to be. Needless to say, my eyes started watering, (a bad habit lately) and my hands shook slightly as I tried to explain myself. It seemed I had come full circle.. it was very weird but it is a moment on this journey that will stay with me!

I rejoined the interstate with about 25 miles to go until Winslow... it went along quickly as I was staring into the distance. Stretching out in front of me was the road, shimmering in the heat, and above that an outline of mountains... these were the mountains of The Grand Canyon and it seemed that I was being drawn towards them, even as they were whispering my name.

I arrived at Winslow, pitched up at a Best Western and set about organising a few things for rest days in Williams, a starting point for many on the visit to The Grand Canyon. I phoned a friend again, and it was with great delight that I have organised to see the canyon with Louize and Mark, who are also bringing me my much needed replacement shorts. A helicopter flight seems to be out of the question at present but I have decided to let my other rest day go where it will take me, although out and about is not in doubt, doing what remains a mystery....

So this evening now has become one for admin, washing clothes, booking my hotel in Wiliams and generally sorting shit out so that I can make the most of my 'rest days' and see some more of this great state.

My card has been marked and all fates collided today leaving me astounded once again!

Despite now having the Grand Canyon for comparison, I still think of the Painted Desert as THE highlight of the ride. There I got to be alone amidst the vastness, if only for 5 minutes, and to experience the peace that being alone in such surroundings generates. I can close my eyes and still feel the effect it had on me.

Chapter 27 - Day 19: Nothing worth having is easily won. Walk on and be strong...

The day began like many others on the road, early start, breakfast, feeling good after the last 2 days that went so smoothly. My foot had stopped hurting when I walked and my knees didn't cause me to groan when I got up from the breakfast table... so far so good.

Once outside, it was reasonably warm, relatively speaking, due to the cloud that had sprung up overnight. It was a bit dreary looking but there was no rain and more importantly no wind.

As soon as I started to cycle though, it quickly became clear that I had either left my legs behind in Winslow or sent them on ahead to Williams, as they weren't keen on pushing on, up out of Winslow and towards my rest days. I also had a possible detour for today, should I think I could make an extra 12 miles and as I groaned up the first hill of the day, I wondered whether it would be a good idea or not.

My detour was about 20 miles away and as I once again headed towards the shadowy outline of the mountains, the cloud and a bit of mist made them seem more mysterious somehow and had dampened the bright colours of the desert scrub to pale imitation yellows, reds and browns.

I reached the turn off point for the detour and made the decision to go for it... and almost immediately regretted it because I was now heading into the wind, going south on a road that was as up and down as anything I had yet encountered. My legs were screaming at me to give up and do the sensible thing of turning round and heading back to I40.. but I pushed on, given that I had already gone 2 miles and it would be for nothing if I didn't reach my goal... so I continued with the bad idea, cursing myself loudly with every increase in gradient. Eventually I reached my destination, to find a hill so steep that even my lowest gears bought little relief.

I had arrived at the meteor crater! Once at the visitors centre, I paid an extortionate amount, especially since it had only cost me $3 to get into the painted desert, and was offered the lift....

Bit of background for those that don't know...

For a leadership course at work I had to lead a change in the workplace... somehow I managed to get a climbing the stairs to work scheme approved, and managed to persuade many (but not all) to take part and climb the 6 flights of stairs to work for 6 weeks...

So knowing what kinda comments I'd get from many of my colleagues if they knew I'd taken the easy option, I climbed the stairs, grinning to myself as I did so... now they would have no excuse good enough (Parker take note!)

At the top, I walked to the rim of the crater and stared down... I had thought it was going to be big obviously, but it was Big! The statue of liberty would easily fit in it, it is so deep. It was pretty impressive....

I was naturally on a time limit and really there is only so much time you can stare at a big hole in the ground... so soon it was time for me to set off again, knowing that I had 6 miles before I was back on track again. This 6 miles was slightly better, being slightly more downhill but with my legs misbehaving, it took a while and a lot of effort to get back to the interstate.

I had thought to myself that it was only another 38 miles to Flagstaff and I could do that by 1pm or so... how wrong I was! Because I had lost quite a few feet since the continental divide, it was now time to regain them.. the road went up and up and up. My legs were gone and with them my head was on the slippery slope to following them. I was in a world of hurt, my foot, which had recovered a bit was now complaining vociferously, the sun was coming out, making me really hot and bothered, although the new venting system in my shorts was working a treat! The mountains were looming larger and the desert like floor was passing me by without so much as a glance because everything hurt. My backside was not liking any position on the saddle and I was constantly shuffling around to try to get comfortable, to no avail. It was not the most pleasant 38 miles I have ever done and I began to wonder whether I would make Williams by nightfall.

Despite the pain, I was still dodging debris, even bits of grass, when I took a closer look.... stick insects everywhere! I stopped right next to one, picked him up, named him Sid and got him to pose reluctantly for a photograph. This done, I released him and set off, now painfully aware that as well as dodging debris and crickets, Sids friends would also have to be avoided. Just as well I was going so slowly. For at least 5 miles this took my mind temporarily of the pain.

During this time I also entered the Coconino forest, which made me laugh, because their version of forest was slightly different to ours... basically slightly taller scrub bushes!

Then Sid's friends were no more and I was back to my bubble of pain for company. I couldn't even sing along to my iPod as due to the increase in altitude that made me out of breath. After what seemed like days I reached the sign that heralded Flagstaff at 2pm... needed food... so stopped at a subway for a pizza.

I felt a bit self conscious walking in... I could hardly walk for a start, my shorts were now more of a waistband with pockets and I have weird tan lines... quite a sight I'm sure, yet once again I encountered nothing but kindness and generosity from everyone. They gave me a free pizza and coffee and asked all about the ride. I had been hoping that a short sit down and food would help me to recover sufficiently to make the last 30 miles... I kept telling myself that after Flagstaff I would be on downhill trend to williams and it would be better..

I rolled, slowly, through Flagstaff, which is nice enough but had nothing that jumped out at me, until I saw a cycle shop....

On the downhills I had had a brake rubbing issue, had adjusted the brakes but was still plagued by the noise... this meant it could be a spoke issue and they needed to be tightened to true the wheel. I could do this, I have the tool but its difficult without a stand to rest the bike on... so I swerved right into the shop, where the kind man adjusted it all, tightened the spokes and then refused payment! Result!

Of course I had to climb out of Flagstaff and the rest hadn't made things any better... I probably could have walked up the hill quicker, but the pedals kept on turning and I gratefully rejoined the interstate. Still climbing up and up though, hardly noticing that I was now going through actual forest, tall pine trees on either side and the late afternoon sunshine pouring through the trees. Had I been in a good place head wise, I would have thought how lovely it was. Eventually I reached a sign proclaiming arrival at the Arizona Divide at 7335 feet. No wonder it had hurt, but did that mean I was going to get my reward for the effort....

I did for about 3 mins as the road plunged downwards on smooth tarmac. Gripping the handlebars at speeds of 31 mph on a loaded bike was fairly adrenaline filled and for those few minutes, everything was good again. I could appreciate the beauty of the view (didn't take a photo, would have ruined the reward!)

I tried desperately to continue the impetus on the uphill sections but my legs felt like stone and soon was back to crawling along...

It was generally better though, with more flat and down than up, but a new problem had arisen... the shoulder had become so broken up, it resembled a dried lava field, and battered my bike about badly. This made me slow down even more, damaging my bike or getting a puncture would have been the last straw at this point.

So the last 30 miles were slow progress, however I had relaxed about getting to Williams before night fell and as a result started to enjoy what I was seeing... the pine forest on either side of the road was being lit up by the evening sun, the clouds were turning red and purple with the sunset and it was the nicest one I have seen since I have been here.

The relief when I got to Williams was so high but once again, there was a sting in the tail of the day.. the road stretched up and over the railway in one last test of the legs. By now it was close to dark and I was desperate to get to the motel... but which one had I booked last night? I hoped I had remembered correctly when I drew up to the door but to my absolute dismay there was a sign with the words closed and a number to ring. When I did, I was directed further back down the road but fortunately it wasn't far.

I collapsed into a decent room with almost no energy left, in fact I found it difficult to turn the door handle I was so tired!

I have blogged a lot about effort and reward, and it occurred to me that I needed another tough day, in order to truly earn and appreciate my 2 days off in Williams and my Grand Canyon visit... which is the thought that has stayed with me for most of the day. I really feel that I have earned every minute I spend in the canyon and it will mean so much more because I have worked hard for it. The same applies to everything in life, I think....

Work colleagues take note.. Climbing the stairs to work scheme was only the beginning!!
Next up... Buscot Bicycle Club

Chapter 28 - Rest Day 2: Life can be beautiful sometimes...

Part 1

Second rest day and it was a bit weird waking up ... (without alarm at 0600) with the knowledge that I didn't have to pack up and get on the road. What the hell was I going to do all day? Well I had some ideas but I wanted to wander around Williams, pick up some more presents, find an ATM, sort out my stuff, catch up with facebook and then see how much time I had left in the day. There was no breakfast offered at this place as far as I could see so I pulled on my shorts, which are on their death bed and wandered down to the diner ....

Sitting at the diner, listening to 60s classic rock and roll hits, drinking coffee, was when I felt myself relax into the day. I had thought of finding something big to do, maybe go to the bear park a few miles out of town, but as I sat here, it was quiet and I felt the need to rush around dissolve into the ether... why not take it a bit easy?

Before I relate about my walk around town, I feel the need to write an obituary...

In memory of black shorts: served their purpose well, eventually worn down until all that was left was a waistband and pockets.. protected modesty for as long as able and new venting system worked well in the heat of the day...

So long, you may be thrown away but never forgotten

Replacement arrives tomorrow!

Having had a great breakfast I wandered up the main street. Williams is a small town and it was pretty quiet this morning, the sun was already shining brightly and I felt so pleased to be here, already beginning to feel the excitement of what tomorrow will bring. The main street of Williams is split into 2 one way streets, next to the railway line that transports people to the Grand canyon. I toyed briefly with the idea of hopping on the train but dismissed the thought as soon as I had it... I really wanted to see the Grand Canyon for the first time with friends and felt it might spoil tomorrow if I went there now, besides all good things come to those who wait, right?

I went into the information centre to ask about where I could comfortably cycle within a few miles of here, to keep the legs going round . I was very glad I did. I saw a t shirt, with the following written on it...

Advice from a canyon
Carve out a place for yourself
Aspire to new plateaus
Stand the test of time
Don't get boxed in
Listen to the voice of the wind
Its ok to be a little off the wall
Reach deep!

It struck a chord with me.. it kinda sums up this journey... needless to say I bought it, which set the tone for the rest of the morning lol.

I also met a lovely lady called Jan, who was very helpful in advice about where I could cycle, some stuff on the route coming up and suggested I head over to Williams newspaper office to tell them about my bike ride and Love Hope Strength Foundation!

I duly did this and spent 15 minutes chatting to a reporter about how I became involved with LHS, what the charity does and about the bike ride... fingers crossed it will help spread the word!

I continued my wanderings, in and out of souvenir shops... by the end of the morning I think I will need some more panniers, every shop I went in I saw a good present for someone! I was even more happy with how the day was turning out after a visit to Addicted to Route 66, where I met several nice gentlemen. Jeremy (hope I have his name right) the shop manager, was very interested in the ride and the charity and we were joined in chat by Al, who had some great insights! When I told him that my friends were worried about me getting killed by an axe murder he said that they needn't worry because around these parts, 'we just shoot them'!

Now in Tulsa I was somewhat surprised to learn that people just walk around with guns, here they most definitely do, because aA pointed out that he was carrying his gun.
On learning how cold I had been on the Texas panhandle he said that people said 'the only thing between the panhandle and the North pole is a barbed wire fence and sometimes even that has been knocked down'!
He was a real character and provided insight into Americans and permits to carry weapons, for example here in Arizona, you don't need a permit as long as you don't plan to do any crime with it... it was very weird for me to try and understand the gun culture that exists here but trying!

Meeting these two people once again made my day... I spent at least half an hour chatting and it was a pleasure to meet them. They also told me that there is a lot of downhill (once I'd climbed up out of Williams of course) which further fueled the belief that I might actually make it. In some ways it feels as though I have, as Williams and the Grand Canyon have been such a big aiming point for me, I have now definitely crossed the highest point, and have reached a big target actually on schedule.

I have to keep reminding myself that I still have over 500 miles still to go until I reach Santa Monica pier.

Also in this shop was a picture of James Dean with the quote
Dream as if you'll live forever
Live as if you'll die today...

Finally from this shop, I've seen the world's largest rocking chair, and now I've seen the world's largest Route 66 sign lol... another to add to my collection.

I spent the rest of the morning wandering round, in and out of souvenir shops, as you do, stopped myself from buying the John Wayne loo roll - its rough, its tough, it doesn't take the crap off of anyone! But added to the weight of the next 500 miles - its all downhill from here, more weight is a good thing..... ?

One of the shops I walked into, Native America, had some beautiful handicrafts made by native americans and it was here that I met 'Sam, I am' who was clearly passionate about the art and crafts in the shop. It was lovely to meet you Sam and I definitely will be back one day!

Eventually I ran back to my motel, mainly in order to avoid spending more dollars. I wrote this half of the blog now, while eating Hershey's (not tired of it yet) and deliberating what to do with the rest of the day. My choices, a short cycle to the Kaibab national forest, to keep the legs going round and stave off the restlessness I am starting to feel, or to the bear park, or just download a film and chill out.. what do you reckon?

Part 2

I was sitting writing the first part of the blog , when there was a knock at the door and a message to phone Sam at the Native American store, i had left something behind.. cursing myself for being careless, I rang the number she had left, spoke to Sam and arranged to drop by on my way out on my bike ride... yup thats right, on my day off I had decided to get back on my bike, mainly to keep my legs in tune for sunday and not seize up. So about half an hour later, I pulled back up to the store and went in, asking Sam what I had been stupid enough to leave behind. Her response surprised me... 'you haven't forgotten anything but I wasn't sure you would come back and I wanted to give you something'. With that she pulled out several beautifully made necklace/wrist chains and asked me to pick one. She explained that they were ghost beads, traditionally given to Navajo children to provide protection from evil spirits. I was so touched by this gesture, yet again a complete stranger had shown generosity and kindness of spirit. This journey has reinforced my faith in human nature, my belief that most people are good and Sam's gesture epitomised that in full. I immediately had them wound round my wrist, which is where they will stay (until I go back to work), hopefully serving their purpose.

Once I had said thank you and goodbye to Sam, I set off to 4th street, where Jan had suggested I go on a cycle ride. My bike was unencumbered by panniers and my rucksack was light. I felt freer than I have on this ride yet, with possibilities opening up as the road stretched out (and of course up) in front of me.

Once i had cleared the houses, a lake with a dam came into view with mountains towering above. The evening sunlight poured down onto the surface of the water, but I kept going, keen to at least put a few miles in today. The road wound up through a pine forest and I was mainly alone on the road. The only sound was my wheels whirring round, the crickets and the birds singing in the evening warmth. I could smell the pine trees which flanked the road and felt somewhat like an intruder on this peaceful scene, like I was disturbing the air through which I rode. I kept onwards and upwards until a couple of miles later, the forest opened out into a golden coloured meadow, shining in the rays of the sun. I stopped still and stood there, breathing in the clean, fresh air, letting it invade my senses.

Eventually I turned round for 2 miles of freewheeling back down to the lake, where I hopped off my bike and set myself down on the shore. The sun was starting to dip behind the mountains and the water was dazzling and rippled in the slight breeze. I had found yet another place on this journey where I could have set myself down forever, it was that enchanting. I sat here, reading my book and watching the sun go down until I got slightly cold, so set off back to town. Before long I found myself in a pizza house, yes Chris S, a pizza house and eyes bigger than stomach ordered a medium size pizza... once again i was unable to finish so boxed it up and went back to the motel... one stop at the fudge shop (sorry mum, couldn't bring any back!) and then sitting writing this.

Tomorrow I get to see the Grand Canyon.. by all accounts it will take my breath away... but surely even this sight will not compare to the kindness and friendship shown by strangers that I have been lucky enough to receive today.

Life is definitely beautiful

The Williams' Post did publish an article which was prtty cool. I liked Williams. Although it was somewhat a 'tourist trap' town it had a charm to it. I could easily have spent a couple of weeks here, exploring the surrounding area, or just sitting by that beautiful lake!

Chapter 29 - Rest Day 3: I breathe the air….

A good friend, Mickey, said to me about today 'live every minute, breathe every breath and take in every heartbeat of scenery'. I hope I did and will try to describe the experience adequately but I fear I will fail...

But first start at the beginning...

I woke up early as usual, keen that today would live up to the expectation. I had everything ready, water, cameras, prayer flags, first aid kit (well it would be typical of me to have come this far and then trip over the edge) and waited for Louize and Mark to come and pick me up. I used to work with Louize and they had moved out here a year ago. On hearing about my trip they had offered to be emergency contacts and we had arranged to meet up. They had kindly offered to take me on a day trip to the Grand Canyon, the point I had been cycling so hard to get to on time to enable me to have a day off for a visit.

Whilst waiting I caught up with facebook, read, played bejeweled, anything to keep me occupied. I felt like a child again, who had woken up too early on christmas day and had to wait to open presents!

Slightly before the agreed time, message of we are here, filtered through and I went out to greet them, in my cycling shorts no less. (My shorts were not fit to wear any more due to having no backside to them whatsoever!) I find it difficult to say how fantastic it was to see someone (technically) from home. Almost as good were the shorts, (and I have just had an oh shit moment as I have realised, in the excitement of the day, I forgot to give them any money for. Louize I will pay you back!) which fitted perfectly and are going to be great to cycle in.

I took them to the diner in which I had breakfast yesterday, and felt almost like a regular. I probably spoke to much and babbled on, due to the fact that I haven't spoken to too many people since being on the road and it was soooo nice to see them. We argued over the cheque, I lost that one, before heading to the car and settling in for the shortish drive. It would have taken me most of the day to get there by bike, but the miles whizzed by, with me still talking 19 to the dozen! Sorry guys!

Before long we pulled up to the park entrance, I won that one, and we drove through to the car park... the weather was glorious, bright blue skies, sun but not too hot, mild breeze... couldn't have been any better. I briefly popped into the visitor centre but seemed funny to be standing there when just outside I could go and see the real thing. We strolled over and suddenly there it was....

It was funny, it didn't hit me at that moment really, but there I actually was. After all these miles....

The first thing I noticed was the beautiful colours in the rock, like the painted desert, perhaps more green in the colours. This stretched down and down and down to the canyon floor, which had more deep gashes in it, presumably where the rivers run, though you couldn't see them. It was so big, the mind cant really comprehend the scale. Between the south rim, where we were and the north rim, were many individual peaks jutting up creating mini canyons within the whole. A sense of the millions of years passing as this canyon was carved out could be felt in your bones.

Now as I was a tourist too, what I'm about to say is slightly hypercritical, but we were surrounded by people and I think that is why it didn't have the initial impact that the painted desert had had on me.. we decided to head down into the canyon on the bright angel trail, which starts off as a reasonably minimal gradient but gets steeper as you go down... it was here that we gradually lost the crowds and descended to a more peaceful place. Here is when I found it hit me, where I was, the significance of how far I had come and more importantly what it meant to me to be taking the flags here.

The flags, on which there are now many names on, have become tied to me and this journey. Many of the people whose names are on these flags, I have never met, but they have become tied to me now as we have shared this journey together. Some are of family who have supported me in this crazy wonderful adventure and some are friends. All are important to me, and I never realised how much until now.

I have carried the flags tied to my bike up until today, when I took them off and carried them around my neck. I was petrified of them blowing away or falling off and continuously was checking that they were safe. I found a good spot and took photos of the individual flags with the words Love Hope and Strength.

With every step down into the canyon I felt more and more the enormity of this place, it dwarfs everything and everyone in it and around it. The walls start to rise up above your head and the drop below still seems a long way down. The strata in the rock mark the passing of millions of years and yet we have barely touched the surface of exploring this place.

I feel pulled downwards, even as I know we must turn back sometime, the trail pulls at my soul, calling me to lose myself in the trees and the rocks below. One day I am determined to come back, with a tent, and keep descending, maybe cross to the other side on foot, but today I must turn back.....

We went slowly back up, it was steep, I was not wearing good walking shoes and the altitude made itself felt. In fact I was wearing the kind of poor quality footwear I often criticise others for wearing up mountains. On top of that I had jarred my injured foot and it was now hurting again. However none of this could take away the magic of this place and when stopped, and the gaze turned once more to the view, it was like seeing it for the first time again, like a reminder that it was still there.

We eventually crested the top and after a well deserved coffee, decided to walk along the rim. At one of the viewing points I stood on a rock with my hands held high, facing the canyon for the photo below. Wham ... it's hit me then, where I was and once again another little piece of me broke away and remained at that spot.. not literally obviously.. don't worry!

The sun was much lower in the sky now, casting shadows in the canyon, giving a greater sense of depth and perspective. If possible it made it look grander, more ancient, more timeless than before. Breathing in the fresh air, smelling the pine that surrounded us and fixing my eye on the view to imprint every moment on my brain, before the bus drew up to ferry us away and back to 'civilisation'.

It was time to go back to Williams but it was not with regret for I am certain that I will come back here to explore and discover more...
We soon found ourselves in an oddly quaint restaurant, with a Swiss chef where I got pasta for the first time in this trip and is of note mainly for the exquisitely prepared apple strudel!

Too soon it was time to say goodbye to Louize and Mark, and face forward, westwards, to LA and the final phase of my journey. I once again had a pang of homesickness for family and friends but restlessness to get going on the road. In Williams I have found kindness and friendship and thanks to Louize and Mark have had a day that will be cherished in my memory.....

So as I prepare for tomorrow I ask that you keep sharing this blog, spreading the word and donating if you feel you can. Your support will propel me the final 500 ish miles as it has carried me to this spot.

If you donate don't forget there is time to add a name to the flags for the final leg to Santa Monica Pier and help support the fantastic work of Love Hope Strength Foundation.. www.justgiving.com/Route66LHS

Mickey's words ring in my ears as ones to continue to live by and as I turn my eyes to the road tomorrow, I will start with a breath of the fresh air around me.

Have you ever been somewhere and it doesn't seem as though you really have?? The Grand Canyon is like that for me. I know I have stood there, I have the pictures to prove it, but it doesn't feel like reality. Maybe because I had been heading towards that point for so long and in my mind it was a huge waypoint in the whole journey, or maybe because it is just too spectacular to absorb at the time.. or maybe it just wants me to go back!!

For any one interested in the fate of my faithful shorts - I left them hanging on the back of a chair in my motel... I was tempted by a weird sentimentality to bring them back with me but weight won over heart in this case.

Chapter 30 - Day 20: The road has a power that creeps into your soul....

0600 Bloody freezing... ok not Texas panhandle freezing but not far off it. Sunrise hasn't happened yet and am all packed and ready to go, but have to wait until 0630 and diner opening time.. bit frustrating but I'm dying and I mean dying for a cup of coffee. This morning I woke up at 0430 to give me enough time to get the last things packed, catch up with facebook etc ... I was so tired, not sure this day off malarkey has done me any good as I feel out of sync with everything and my body has decided that it quite liked doing nothing for a day or two!

So there I was waiting for this diner to open, knowing that my day consisted of two parts... 40 miles to Seligman on the interstate, then leave the interstate to take the loop of Route 66 up to Peach Springs.

It was all downhill from now right! Having had breakfast the first climb of the day was up and out of Williams. I felt a tinge of sadness leaving this place, the only place I have stayed in this long, but glad to be back on the road... I had missed the whirring of my wheels, the exhilaration of descents and even the struggle of the climbs. As soon as I started out, something was wrong... not a puncture this time, but the feel, the balance of it. Its difficult to describe to non cyclists, but its like when you think there might be ice on the road, and you don't quite trust your car as much in the corners or when braking. Sometimes it happens for a bit when you get a new bike and it handles slightly differently, not so you could explain how, it just doesn't feel the same. Perhaps I'd packed my panniers slightly differently or maybe the weight of souvenirs was unbalancing my bike... it felt skittish, which is ok going slowly uphill....

..... but not so great on the first downhill of the day (I know I know, never happy right). It didn't help that as promised this was a long downhill section, with a steep gradient and that somewhere in the recesses of my mind I was thinking about the overturned lorry a few weeks back. I had a choice, just go with the hill and get it over and done with or go really really slowly. I chickened out and went slowly, brakes on close to full. Now any cyclists out there laughing at me... its one thing to descend at 50 mph on a light road bike, another with a stable loaded bike at 30mph and quite another prospect altogether when your bike feels unstable on the flat!

So I went down at about 14mph, half speed basically, and not only that but the descent absolutely froze me, and now we are talking panhandle frozen. In the space of about 15 miles I descended close to 2000 feet and by the time I got to the bottom I was shivering uncontrollably. Ok so I should have probably put on my gloves and windproof before the descent, not after, but you live and learn and frankly I'd been pretty scared so was happy with the living part!

As any cyclist worth their lycra knows, what goes down, must and invariably does go up and passing up through Ash fork on the way to Seligman, I was actually relieved not to be descending. Ash fork is a very small town, with 1 monument to Route 66 that I saw, and that's pretty much it... so before long I was again on the interstate, climbing slowly westwards. Fortunately the sun had started to heat up the day and with every foot I had descended it got noticeably warmer so that soon I was pretty warm.

The other advantage of descending is that I could once again sing along to my iPod... it has been a pretty good judge of how high I am.. above 6000 feet, cant sing and cycle... below is all good, unless you happen to be some poor passer by!
This invariably cheers me up, loudly singing along to Drunk and Disorderly and Another Country etc.
Seligman appeared very quickly.. it had taken me just under 3 hours to cover 40 miles, which with picture stops isn't bad.

Seligman is apparently where Route 66 began and is basically a street full of gift shops and cafés proudly displaying the Route 66 logo. I stopped in the Roadrunner cafe, happy because it was just 11 am and I had already done half distance!

I got coffee and a snack and wandered round the gift shop... to my delight saw nothing I wanted to buy, either for myself or someone else and left without adding to my pannier weight. I also didn't stop at any other shops, except to take a picture of the roadkill cafe, where apparently they will cook any fresh roadkill you bring in....

So onto the old Route 66 road, and to my surprise it was in good condition but, yup, you guessed it, it went up and up, and up. Not steeply but climbing nonetheless but given that I wasn't stressed about making it to Peach Springs before dark and the scenery was so pretty, none of this mattered. Basically this part of the route kinda follows the rim of the Grand Canyon and it is reasonably close, but what made it so good to stare at was the shining golden colour of the desert grass that set off the bright blue sky. Every now and then at the top of a small descent I would get a glimpse of the valley I was heading towards with more mountains in the distance. The air was fresh with a slightly cool breeze and I was pretty happy with life. Scary descents long forgotten, I was getting the feel of this different machine and gaining more confidence in it on the short descents....

I didn't take many photos basically because it would have been pretty much the same photo, but hope they give an idea. Whilst I was cycling along, every 10 to 15 minutes a car would drive by, often with the driver turning to look at me mouth agape... I find this really funny, don't they ever see people on a bike? It got me thinking about my mode of transport though and why I love it so much, and why I cant understand why people think its crazy to cycle across the U.S.A. These people in their cars are often on their mobiles, or just gazing at the road ahead, oblivious to the work of art that surrounds them... okay, they might get to stop at all the tourist attractions, but why pay to see something when you are surrounded by beauty (Grand Canyon the exception) and even if they do occasionally glance out of their side window, do you really appreciate the view as much if you cant breathe in the fresh air and smell the fresh grass... I don't think you can, and finally I think it goes back to my previous blog statement of nothing worth having is easily won... I know how much more I appreciate a view across a valley if I have put in the effort to get up a hill to see it!

Now today has been a pretty easy day right? Only 80 miles, some downhill and no wind... well that would be correct if it wasn't for the other problem. At the risk of embarrassing some of you, I feel it is only right to share the bad bits as well as the good, and the following is a fact of life for cyclists... chafing... not good. Couldn't sit on the saddle for more than 5 mins in the last 20 miles, which led to more stops and the last 10 miles took twice as long as they should have. Maybe this is why professionals have 3 week long grand tours and not 4. It wasn't a huge problem today with such short mileage but the next 2 days could be long anyway without having to deal with that...oh well, just have to see how it goes I suppose!

I pulled up to Peach Springs at 1530, to find the one and only place to stay... Hulapai lodge, which cost an arm and a leg..

even with the armed forces discount they gave me.. still it is a nice room, good early breakfast, a fitness room opposite my room... which led me to thinking.... more about that possibly later!

So another day done and after 2 rest days, fantastic as they were, especially thanks to Louize and Mark, the road has crept into my soul and I'm glad to be heading westwards on it once again.

I never did come back to the fitness room part of this day... my intention was to sit there and complete the 'missing 20'. Unfortunately all the equipment was switched off, thwarting my grand scheme of making up the mileage
The other problem I had (minor) was that constantly heading westwards had left me with a very tanned/burnt left leg and a less tanned/burnt right leg. It had got so ridiculous that whenever I stopped I tried to stand eastwards facing to even things up... it did not work!

Chapter 31 - Day 21: From the highest of highs to the lowest of lows....

Sticking my feet out of the door from breakfast was enough to tell me the weather had changed.... specifically the wind was up. A second longer look outside gave me the sinking feeling... it was strong and was most definitely not a tailwind. At least it wasn't cold.. but having learnt my lesson the other day, on went the gloves and wind jacket anyway and with that I put my head to the wind.

I had plans for the day... to cover 100 ish miles to the state boarder and not least meet up for lunch with Monica, a likeminded Alarm fan who had been in touch via facebook once she heard my journey was going to take me through her hometown....

Arizona had other ideas. Once again a state had decided not to let me go easily... either that or this was so I had truly earned Santa Monica pier. So Arizona let the headwinds rip. The first 30 miles to Kingman were without doubt the worst I have ever experienced on a bike. Worse than New Mexico. Initially I managed 8 miles per hour but as the hours went past 6 was the best it got. The scenery... nope cant tell you much about that as my eyes were fixed to the tarmac and my teeth were gritted. When I did look up it was into a haze of dust that the wind had kicked up. The first 10 miles were either into a headwind or a sidewind, so vicious that several times I was almost blown off my bike.

These conditions had the advantage of making me forget the small problems from yesterday.

It is here that I will introduce you to the concept of catch up miles because for about 5 miles I was lucky enough that the road turned, turning the sidewind into a tailwind for a brief, hopeful moment. Catch up miles are where you have been going slowly for some reason, be it bad road surface, headwind, or gradient. Then for a period of time, conditions improve. This is where you must go down to the drops, put your head down and put as much effort in as possible to go as far and as fast as possible before the conditions change for the worse again. So for those few delightful miles, I was racketing along at 20 mph... didn't stop and because I knew the route, I knew I would be facing this headwind for the rest of the day.

The last 10 miles of this stretch, into Kingman, I could barely reach walking pace (you know its not great when the tumbleweed is hurtling straight at you) and was getting mouthfuls of dust that had been kicked up. I must have looked so wretched that a kind lady in her truck, offered me her condolences (she had done some cycling) and offered me a lift into town. I explained why I couldn't, at which point she apologised that she didn't have any food or drink to give me... This encounter buoyed my spirits for the next 5 mins, by which time I was back to shouting obscenities at the wind. The sign for Macdonalds was a welcome sight, even though it must have taken me 15 mins to cover a few hundred yards, so strong was the wind at this point. I sunk into a Dennys, absolutely exhausted. Every fibre of my being had just about reached breaking point and then stretched beyond it. More than that, I couldn't see how on earth I was going to get to Oatman, where Monica lived, before dark, never mind the border.

I phoned Monica, trying to convert a plan a to plan b in my head. Now Monica and I had never met, but without hesitation, she offered me a bed for the night if I could get to Oatman, as there is no motel there. I was so grateful for the offer, as it meant I didn't have to stop in Kingman or put any other plan in my head, into action. If I stopped at Oatman, I would be a little short on miles but not as disastrously as it could be and with a better day tomorrow, I might make up time.

I knew it was the right decision when a kind gentleman told me that the winds would be better tomorrow.

So having eaten, and some determination restored, I set off again, knowing that the next 30 would probably be as bad... I wasn't disappointed. I knew thanks to Monica, that I had about 20 miles of flat before a steep climb over the pass. Which would have been fine, if the wind hadn't continued to gust, (apparently up to 55mph). The road wasn't great condition either, which didn't help, and I continued to struggle onwards, hitting the lowest I had felt this entire trip. I kept the pedals turning, occasionally stopping to try to admire the view. As got closer to the mountains, the desert floor got more rockier and less sandy than previous, and I kept my eye out for interesting creatures, even hopping off my bike and going back to photograph a (dead) snake!

Losing the will, I made it to the foot of the pass. The climbing was ok, and once in amongst the mountains, I was somewhat sheltered from the wind...but it was all taking too much time and sunset was fast approaching.

The road wound up the side of the mountain rocks, no barrier in many places so was being extra careful. About half way up I stopped at a gift shop (lol) and met George the manager, who was kind enough to give me a coke and offer me a chair, but not before calling me crazy!

I only sat for 5 mins, aware time was ticking on and pushed on. The road was stunning with mountains towering to either side, but as I finally reached the top, the sun was dropping behind the horizon. Downhill catch up time right... eerrr nope. The gradient was steep, I had my brakes on full and was picking my way round the u turn bends. By this time it was getting hard to see, so eventually as night fell, I got off my bike.

I knew Oatman wasn't that far and it was becoming dangerous to continue on the descent. So I walked the final 2 miles, until I saw lights in the road, and Monica calling out my name. Man was I grateful!

Monica turned out to be a bubbly kindhearted person, who made me feel so welcome in her home, and along with her children and her husband, deserves a medal for just accepting a stranger into their midst for the night. Not only that but I got to see all their pets, including loads of small frogs.... very cool.

As I write this I am knackered and desperate to sleep, knowing it will be another long day tomorrow.. the forecast is supposed to be better tho and I remain hopeful. So another day done, catch up hopefully tomorrow, then just 2 more days of this crazy adventure!

So I hit the lowest of the low, but maybe for good reason, cos I got to spend time with Monica and get to know her, instead of the quick coffee planned... fingers crossed for tomorrow... nite all

This was the closest I came to getting out my tent. The headwinds absolutely destroyed me. It all worked out well in the end though as things often do and looking back on it wasn't as disasterous for my schedule as it felt at the time. It is funny though, the image I have as Monica would have seen me... stumbling out of the dark, pushing my bike along. Such a contrast from the previous day's elation. On a better day with more time and less miles, the climb and descent could have been a very rewarding cycle ride, such was the scenery, but once again maybe the appreciation would have been lessened if it had been easy.

Chapter 32 - Day 22: Try to stop me, I will carry on….

Thanks to Dave for the inspiration for todays blog title and the song which kept me pedalling today.

This is my second version of this blog as I had no wifi last night and then technical issues with blogspot so this version is with 24 hours of hindsight.

You may remember that I had a torrid time on day 21, which led me to crawl in to Oatman after dark, thankfully welcomed by Monica and her family for which I am very grateful. I hadn't seen any of Oatman in the dark so before I set off we had pictures in front of the painted wall.

It was lovely to meet a fellow alarm fan but once again I turned my eyes westwards. Because of the shortfall in mileage, today I had to cycle 114 miles as there is NOTHING between Needles and Ludlow except desert.

Thankfully the winds had died down and as Monica had told me, the road to Needles was good downhill most of the way. It was pretty cold and my legs didn't feel as though they belonged to me after yesterdays battering, but as it was easy for the first 23 miles, I didn't notice the screaming yet!

I was disappointed not to see any of the donkeys that roam wild but I did see a roadrunner as it sprinted across my path, and before anyone asks, no unfortunately he was not followed by coyote!

So I stopped in Needles for a second breakfast, knowing that this was it, until I got to Ludlow. At the subway there, I met 2 lovely women, who showed an interest in my ride and wished me well for the journey. I also stocked up on sugar for the remainder of the day. Then the hard work began. I finally saw the Colorado River, and here, calm and serene, it showed nothing of the immense power that carved out the Grand Canyon.

I realised that I had entered California, there was no fanfare, no grand entrance and accordingly no emotional reaction to entering my 8th and last state, very low key.

The next 40 miles were tough, uphill most of the way and pain all over. My mood was low and even if a den of rattlesnakes had stood up and applauded my effort, I wouldn't have noticed, I was so wrapped in my world of hurt. I was going very slowly and didn't really notice the scenery, though I did occasionally glance at the mountains that surrounded me. And so it went on, and on and on. I despaired of making it to Ludlow and mentally prepared myself for spending the night in the desert. Then my iPod died...... things could not have been worse

Then with about 40 miles to go, I remembered the song lyrics that Dave had reminded me of.., Try to stop me, I will carry on, try to oppose me, I will prevail. A wave of determination came over me and the legs started working better... the next 20 miles were better, as I wavered between despair and determination. I'm not telling you this to gain anything, rather I want to show that even when you think you cant do any more, or continue any further, you can... whatever it may apply to in life and anyone can do it.

So the final 20 miles....determination won, and I put my head down and tried to time trial my way to the end. The mountains were beautiful in the evening light and as the sun started to dip behind them, the desert shone with a purple hue, with the outline of the mountains behind. I continued to push my legs beyond what I though I could as painfully the amount of miles left until Ludlow crept downwards. Aided by (finally) some downhill and a slight tailwind, it was just getting to the point where I couldn't see the road, when the turnoff arrived.

Now hoping that the motel was open, I crawled over to it, it appeared shut! Fortunately some kind soul directed me to the gas station, where the keys were held. I was informed that there was no wifi, but they kinda had me over a barrel, so I had no choice but to accept.

I missed updating facebook and catching up with everyone from home, but 114 miles done, caught up to schedule again and I had prevailed - just.

Just to highlight the kindness of strangers on the way, one of the ladies I met at the Needles' gas station subsequently donated to the bike ride.

The song that inspired me on this day, 'Without a fight' was just one of many songs with inspirational lyrics by Mike Peters, that provided impetus for me to keep going. The power of music on the mind and body is an amazing thing and for me an essential part of daily life.

Chapter 33 - Day 23: Give me Love Hope and Strength...

I was pretty knackered this morning... 2 tough days in a row had left me physically exhausted... not having the chance to catch up with friends had left me mentally low. I knew I had a long day and having had breakfast I checked my tyre again... it had needed blowing up quite a bit yesterday and I thought I might have a slow puncture. Once again this morning, I inflated it, wondering whether to just change the inner tube but as it seemed to be holding, I set off. It was fairly cold but with my wind jacket on, and the usual uphill climb I got very warm pretty quickly.

The next place along was Newberry Springs, 25 miles down the road and I took the interstate after being advised that the Route66 highway was pretty bumpy until Newberry springs when the road condition improved. For once I did not have road envy, as the interstate shoulder was smooth. I wasn't sure whether I was going slowly because of my back tyre, the slight headwind or the uphill gradient. Probably a bit of all three, but it seemed to take forever to reach the town.

On the way, I noticed that the desert was becoming sandier, with less rock and brush and tried to distract myself by letting my mind wonder. This is what I like about cycling, it leaves the mind free and thoughts roll through like the wheels rolling on the tarmac. Also it distracts from any discomfort you may be feeling. I thought about my family, friends, how fortunate I am, how I might feel if I get to the pier tomorrow... a million different shards all splintering in my head.

Eventually Newberry Springs came into sight and I stopped to eat, hoping that wifi would be available... nope, no catch up.

After this the next 30 miles to Barstow were tough but at least I was on the old Route 66, actually cycling through the desert, searching (in vain) for snakes and spiders. It was a nice road, with only the occasional car passing. At one point I was directed to the other side of the interstate, but having consulted my off line maps, decided to continue on this road, only to find myself at a checkpoint for a marine corps logistics base... I could pass, but they would have to search my bags... don't think so... so turned round and jumped back on the interstate! I saw a few lizards running away from my wheels here as well, which made the detour worthwhile.

I got to Barstow quicker than I thought I would and although it was fairly busy (since Ive got used to quiet country towns) , it was quite a nice place and suddenly it hit me that I was in California and tomorrow (hopefully) would be the end! More tears (got to stop that) as I realised how far I'd come, and how close I was....

I found a Starbucks and oh joy of joys could finally catch up with home... all the messages of support buoyed my mood no end and by the time I set off again, the remaining 40 miles of the day, seemed a mere hop and my legs felt light again.... this is how important the support has been to me, how it has kept my legs turning round and got me to the edge of LA. Without it I would have ground to a halt long ago!

Those final miles were on the Route 66 road and I had been pre warned that it had been freshly tarmacked (thanks faith), so I knew to be careful. Thankfully it had bedded down a bit, and there wasn't too much loose gravel around.

I stopped at the bottle forest, a collection of bottles, mounted like branches on poles, topped with all kinds of recycled items. The owner came out and told me that he had built it over 14 years... it really was a work of art and well worth stopping for. The last 15 miles were reasonable, winding up, before dropping down into Victorville. I made my way to the motel I had been recommended (up a hill of course) and the manager kindly upgraded me to a suite, after discussing the merits of Sidcup where he had once lived! So I sit writing this in luxury lol.

I then had the pleasure of the company of two lovely people, Don and Kimberly, who took me out to dinner. It was lovely to meet them and I hope to see you at the gig on Friday! Thank you!

So another day done, one which saw the power that Love Hope and Strength from friends can have to a knackered, leg weary, slightly homesick cyclist.... Roll on tomorrow...

Don and Kimberley did come to the gig on the Friday night, which was absolutely fantastic. Once again, and I will not tire of saying this, the generosity, kindness and support of people who before had been complete strangers amazed me. Faith in the human race has been well and truly restored. What I didn't mention about the meal is that it was big enough for 4 people and that didn't include the side salad! I managed barely to dent it and didn't even have room for one of the tempting banana splits that were on display on other tables!

Chapter 34 - Day 24: Here I stand....

I thought I would start todays blog last night as I'm not sure what state I'm going to be in, should I get to the pier in 1 piece. So to make sure I say everything I wanted to say and risk boring you all, the first half of this blog is reflection of the journey the night before.

Part 1

First and foremost this ride has been for the people whose names are on my prayer flags. They are family, friends and people I have never met but all have been tied to me and shared every step of this adventure with me. They are (in no particular order) :

Dave Spragg
Mitch Dooley
Stevie Collins
Vera Collins
Peter Collins
Peter Sirett
Marija Milinkovic
Eric Ray
Gordon Wilson
Anne Wilson
Tom Lloyd Twitchen
Hazel Rolf
George Rolf
Richard Tankard
Irene Burns
Kamila
Laura

Sue Jones
Melanie Sykes
Harris Shryock
Darren Clark
Viv Pugh
Norman Winn
Mickey Collins
Scott Weten Kemp
Kelly Lick
Frances Catt
Ken Owens
Ladda
Reuben Graham
Mike Peters
Monica Thompson
Irene Wyeth
Damien Blake
Tinie
Gwen
Denise Falcus
Irene Mulloy
Henry Mulloy
Annabel
Sam
Mandy Setterfield
Judith Brown
Sara Williams
Urszula Smith
Jean Kavangh
Una Quinn
Jill Yates
Celia Wilson
Melvin Wilson
Paul Wilson

Jean Ford
Sandie Ford

I described this journey in the beginning as solo and unsupported, and in so much as I have been physically alone, it was by no means unsupported. I cannot name everyone who has commented on my blogs or donated as I would wish to, but special thanks go to (again in no particular order):

My family - Thank you for your support of all things crazy
My work mothers - for putting up with me and messages of encouragement
Mickey for his phone calls when I have been low and general motivation, you are an official legend
Mike and Jules Peters and family for the inspiration, encouragement, and music!
Dave Spragg - for friendship
Emma Dunne, especially for phone call when homesick
Beki and Randy - for friendship and support
Joe Silva- for being awesome and the support
Kelly Dooley Creek - for organising help and support
Louize and Mark Evans - for shorts and showing me the Grand Canyon
Monica Thompson - for letting me crash unexpectedly
Faith - for taking interest In a stranger and the journey
Buscot ward - for cake eating, climbing the stairs, support and helping to provide a great place to work
David Vieira - for kindly donating the gig venue
Helen Simons and family - for welcoming me and helping getting me organised at the scary beginning part
Rob Rushing - for sharing, support and swabbing fun!
James Chippendale - for your enthusiasm and support.
Sophie Franklin - for being the best kind of best friend.

Everyone who has sent messages of encouragement, support, inspiration and donated... could not have done it without ya x

So thats the Oscar Speech out of the way.....

Together we have raised over £3800 and hopefully more from the gig..
I have cycled over 2300 miles, burnt 96000 calories (at best guess), renewed my faith in humanity and made new friends.

My favourite part of the ride (excluding the finish) has been sitting at the edge of the painted desert, breathing the air and listening to the wind.
My worst day is a toss up between headwind day in New Mexico and headwind day in Arizona.
I have learnt that I can keep going long past the point where I thought I was done for.
I have had 2 real scrapes with injury or worse but have seized many many opportunities to really live.
My fingers do not work properly and my foot is screwed up.
I have lived every minute, breathed every breath and taken in every heartbeat along the way

Love Hope Strength Foundation together with delete blood cancer swabs people for the bone marrow donor list to help save lives... if you have enjoyed this blog, please consider Getting on the list - it takes 5 mins and you could help save a life... please go to www.deletebloodcancer.org.uk to get a home kit! If you have not donated to the ride and feel able to contribute, please go to www.justgiving.com/Route66LHS and help get the total to over £4000!

LHS was founded by Mike Peters of The Alarm and James Chippendale. Both are legends and Mike never ceases to amaze me with his boundless energy and enthusiasm. He is my inspiration and his music has kept my pedals turning round day after day. Huge thanks to them and Jules Peters for allowing me to be a small part of the whirlwind!

Finally, please note that anyone could have done this... YOU could have done this... you can do anything you want to, you just have to make the choice...

Part 2

It was kinda weird packing up this morning, knowing that this would, if all went to plan, be the last day of this journey. I had everything ready to go for the moment it got light as wanted to get through the pass before traffic got really bad.,
As I set off, the usual heavy legged feeling was there, but I tried to tell myself that they had felt like that every day at the start. I was still worried about my back tyre, convinced I had a slow puncture but it felt ok, but I was cursing myself for not changing the inner tube as a precaution.

I followed the frontage road, looking for the freeway entrance that would then take me through the hills and when I found it, hopped on. The first problem of the day struck... the shoulder was closed for two miles and by closed I mean walled off not just coned off, so I was actually in a lane... not a good plan at all... if I was to survive today, I had to find another way. I pulled in at the works entrance and chatted to the foreman, who directed me to a side road that had just been re-tarmacked, saying that it led back to the Mojave freeway, which cut through the hills surrounding LA and is the only way through. Result ... smooth, fast, all good. Didn't last long though and before long I was back on the freeway.

Mojave freeway has steep descents of 6% where lorries are advised to stop and check their brakes, and there are frequent signs for escape lanes for the lorries... none of this boded well. To top it all off, the shoulder had bumps every 20 meters. So there I was, standing up on my pedals to be seen better, being shaken to the bone, brakes on to keep my speed reasonable and hoping that I would live to see LA. Fortunately all the drivers seemed to be taking the warnings seriously and for the most part, drove sensibly. It was still a hell of an adrenaline rush though.

12 hair raising miles later,I was directed off to the old Route 66 road... and it was a true pleasure to cycle... dropping down through the hills in a reasonable road, quiet with just a goods train for company. I really enjoyed it. The road then wound under the freeway to a lovely rural community. Then it was onwards, waiting at the tracks for the train to pass the crossing, and up to the old Route 66.

I was burning by this time, the sun was beating down, and I was starting to get stopped by traffic lights which was slowing me down. As my legs had warmed up, the pace had improved and I was struck by the wide roads, with proper bike lanes (UK take note, they didn't stop after 50 meters) and Spanish looking villas with immaculate sculpted gardens. The workmen were out with the leaf blowers and hedge trimmers and it was very pleasant to cycle through.

Up to this point I had been concentrating on not getting mown down, so I hadn't really thought about where I was and how close I was, this was the first time (of several) that it hit me smack in the face.... oh nope, that was the bees or wasps on this part of the road who weren't concentrating on where they were going as I got torpedoed by several of them, so much so that I made a concerted effort to keep my mouth shut as I cycled along... I could see the headlines... "charity cyclist dies after being stung at the back of the throat by a wasp with a misguided sense of direction"! Fortunately the wasp/bee storm was over pretty quickly and I started dropping down through the various towns in the suburbs of LA.

I liked these places, particularly Duarte, Fortuna, Claremont and Arcadia, each with their own personality and feel to them. I thought that if this was LA, I could see why people liked it here.

The road ran on and crossed over the freeway. A motorbike drew up alongside and asked about my ride, so I explained. He commented on how thin my tyres were, then wished me a safe journey. 20 or maybe 30 seconds later, there was a clang of something metal, a pop and a rear puncture. I actually laughed at the timing of this and without too much concern sat down at the edge of the road and replaced the inner tube... 45 minutes this time (you may recall it was an hour last time) and as I had been making good progress, I thought I would still be fine for time.

I phoned Beki, just to update on progress and then went on my way, still feeling pretty good. It wasn't to last... as I dropped even further down towards LA City center, I got cut up by a bus and then my front tyre went flat!
REALLY??? It felt a bit like everything was trying to stop me getting to the pier today. So once again, I sat down and repaired the damage. The main problem being that this was my last inner tube and one more puncture had the capacity to ruin everything. I kept the old inner tube in case I needed to patch it up, and although this one took 30 mins to mend, I was now looking at a very long afternoon with 62 miles minimum to go.

As I reached the centre, I was struck once again by where I was and choked back the tears, telling myself I wasn't there yet! Then a right turn onto Sunset Boulevard and a long drag up to find the turning for Santa Monica boulevard and my path to the pier and the end of the ride.

It was starting to get late and I was getting concerned about what time I would get to the pier,. With punctures and traffic lights I was now looking at a 6pm arrival. I began to get frustrated with the lights as I was stopping very frequently and couldn't hold a good speed because of it. I was aware Beki and Randy were waiting for me, and didn't want to cycle in the dark much!

I asked some 'cops' on bikes how far and they gave me news of at least 2 hours, which made my heart sink. 19:30 arrival in darkness beckoned.

I continued on, turned into Santa Monica blvd and got my lights on as starting to get dark. Then the weirdest thing happened... I stumbled upon a zombie, then a vampire, a ghost... the road had been closed for a Halloween festival so I spent a few happy minutes dodging pedestrians instead of cars and laughed at the random event on this ride which made the day. It was by now pretty dark and I was fairly nervous, especially as the cops had warned me about the large amount of drunk drivers out on the road. I cycle in the dark at home obviously but it is completely different doing that in a strange city. I stopped at some lights when a cyclist pulled up alongside, asked if I was ok (musta looked petrified lol) and where I was headed. He then offered to cycle with me to the pier. Which made the last 6 miles much nicer... 2 bikes are better than 1, especially when 1 knows the city and therefore I finished up at the entrance to the pier, alive, unhurt and safe. So grateful to him for doing that...

So I was at the pier entrance.. phoned Beki... "we are waiting at the sign on the pier" came the reply... only another 200 meters to go... up the slope and down the other side... to a chorus of cheers and clapping! Beki and Randy had rounded up a load of random English people to see me to the end! What a lovely thought!

No tears... even I was surprised given my recent affliction of crying at every emotional moment. But I was shaking quite a bit...

Big hugs from Beki and Randy... how absolutely fantastic to be able to share this moment with some friends.

Then it was photo time, although I had ruined all photo plans by arriving in the dark, which made it tricky. With the help of a flashlight provided by a cop, I have a record of me at the end of the road, with the flags! (I will take photos of the individual flags and names at the gig tomorrow night.)

A phone call from friends on a night shift completed the day!

Food, at an English pub (to help with my homesickness) then to the travel lodge and facebook catch up.

I plan to blog about tomorrow, so the journey is not quite done.

I wondered about how to finish off todays blog, there seemed only one fitting way:

With Love, Hope and Strength.

Chapter 35 - Gig day: I'm made of life...

Today was the day... the celebration of the End of the ride at Rock and Roll Pizza in Moorpark.

It didn't get off to a great start... I went to have breakfast (must get back out of that habit) and discovered that there had been a shooting at the airport which is just down the road from where I am staying. Typical, I arrive safely after cycling across the country and there is a shooting nearby lol. Obviously in no danger but all the roads were blocked by police, fire trucks and ambulances on a day when I had a gig to get too! Beki and Randy were picking me up early afternoon and we weren't sure whether they would be able to get near my hotel or whether I would have to walk out.

5 news choppers were hovering overhead and every few minutes a police car or firetruck would come racing down the road, sirens blaring. . It was like seeing a live action movie. I stayed outside, I guess kind of fascinated by the ongoings. Eventually I wandered back and switched the tv channel to CNN. Reports of gunmen, injuries and panic were ongoing. The situation was fluid though and It shows that there is no need to stress about something until it actually happens and the roads opened just in time and Beki and Randy walked through the door of the lobby with plenty of time to make our way north for the gig in Moorpark.

We checked into a hotel nearer the gig and the lack of effort in getting there meant I had ample time to appreciate the scenery. California is a lovely state, with mountains and permanent blue sky and sunshine... it is a shame that I haven't had more time here.

On arrival at the Rock and Roll Pizza photos by the sign were a must and then we wandered in. The venue is filled with rock and roll including a drum skin that Mike Peters had signed - surely the best bit in the place I think. The next hours were filled with meeting new people, greeting friends and a whirlwind of thoughts. I will try and describe a few key moments in the evening.

Beki and Randy took to the stage and I hadn't heard a full set before... the original songs grasped me immediately, with lyrics that were at once intriguing and memorable... I have only spent bits of time with them before but both of them along with Floyd and Christie, Kelly and Mary provided a solid foundation for the feeling that here I was amongst friends. It made the homesickness lessen, as we caught up from the last time we met and this is what I love about The Alarm and LHS, the fact it has enabled me to meet people like this and feel as though I have known them forever. Thank you to all!

Amongst the crowds of people were Lee and his family, on holiday from the UK, who had come along to support, it was great meeting them and comparing notes on weird things in the U.S.A. Also Don and Kimberly, who I had met in Victorville, took time out to come and support and amazingly rendered me speechless with a generous donation to the ride, so great to have you guys there.

Alan R also stunned me with a gift of a coin made for Everest rocks which he took part in. It meant a huge amount to me and it is safe in my pocket..

Joe Silva's set was full of my favourite songs of his and as usual he played from the heart. Joe was one of the first people to jump in and support this ride from the beginning and it was so great to see him play again. His album blue, is well worth downloading and has many songs you will find yourself singing along to..Check it out! Thanks also to Joe, for saying something that made me stop and think about where I had started from and how this had all come together... it made the gig special.

My favourite part of the gig was the moment where me, Joe and Beki gave a rousing rendition of Love, Hope and Strength, to an audience that joined in, when they didn't know the song... it was a special moment for me and the word is being spread!

Chevy metal, to be honest were not necessarily my cup of tea but I went down the front at the end, got some photos for people back home, who are big fans, and enjoyed the moment. It was also see great to see Joe invited up to drum, whilst Taylor sat at the side of the stage! Thats rock and roll for you!

More importantly perhaps, the Love Hope Strength team had been working tirelessly under the tent and signed up 23 people to the bone marrow donor list... a great result and one that put the icing on the cake for me.

When the end arrived, it had seemed such a short time as as I said goodbye to various friends, it all seemed a bit surreal. Many I will see again soon though (Floyd, about the gathering...) and for a short while Rock and Roll Pizza had become a part of home for me.

So fast forward (so I don't bore you)... oh but before I do, I must tell you that although I managed to get from Chicago to LA injury free, I tripped over in the parking lot and got bloody road rash down my right leg... lol

So fast forward to this morning.. I enjoyed a pile of pancakes with strawberries and bananas for breakfast and then beki and randy dropped me off at terminal 7 to find a box for my bike... passed around from place to place, where I met the most unhelpful people of this whole trip... the conversation went something like this..

Me :can I buy a box for my bike

Them: we don't have any

Me: well can I check it in without one

Them: no, we don't accept bikes without boxes

Me: well can you suggest what I should do

Them: most people bring a box

Me: well I just cycled from Chicago so it would have been difficult

Them: you need a box

So mentally preparing myself to abandon my bike in the airport and quite possibly set off another major security alert I phoned a friend.. specifically Beki.

To cut a long story shorter, Beki was a legend, found a bike shop, specifically Performance Bicycle in Torrence, where they sorted out a box and some packaging, which Beki then dropped off to me, and became a bike roadie, whilst I took off the saddle, handlebars and pedals and successfully shoved the bike in its box... result.. so once again, thank you to Beki, for ensuring that the bike that got me safely here could come back with me!

Whilst I was waiting for Beki, I had a moment where I thought bloody hell, I did it. And mixed in there was a sadness to leave the road behind, if only for a while, and leave all my friends here behind, even if also only for a while..

But I'm lucky in my life that I have family and friends to return to, a job I love and a Big Country gig or 2, where I will be helping to swab people for the bone marrow donor list, and no doubt jumping up and down to The Journey!

Thank you to everyone who has supported me, together the rough total is around £6500 raised and I'm so grateful to all who have shared this with me.

'What we do in life always echoes inside' - so Dream Aloud, Fight Back and Stay Alive!

The moment where I crested the rise of the bridge that led to the pier, the last few hundred yards, seeing Randy and then Beki and finally coming to a halt just below the Route 66 sign, still feel as though they happened to someone else. I remember feeling disorientated at the time but there was no huge inner whoop of joy, just disbelief that I was actually there. When Randy asked me what I wanted to do next, I didn't know. Probably because this was where my plans and dreams had ended and I hadn't got any plans for what happened once I got there. I had been living from day to day on a strict schedule with little room for abstract decisions and so it felt really abnormal to be given such choices. I was also totally knackered!!

Over 2 weeks later, it still hasn't sunk in. I have had fleeting moments where I have felt a burst of satisfaction, more to do with the amount raised than by completing the ride, but no real pride in my achievement. Others may think that this is strange and I'm struggling myself to understand why the whole thing hasn't hit me more yet. So answers on a postcard to....

Chapter 36 - Homecoming to Love Hope and Strength...

When I left off from the last blog.. I was at LAX waiting to get on the plane to come home. Its difficult to describe the feelings I had at that point. It all seemed a bit surreal really, and I felt weird not being on the road.

I was sad to say goodbye to my friends here but it was time to be at home. I love having adventures but at the end of the day, home, Reading and my workplace is where I really belong.

I landed at Heathrow to a lovely (low key as ordered) arrival and lunch with my parents, my brother and Emma. Finally got rid of some of the presents that I had been hauling around for weeks lol, and caught up.

It was funny, I'd start to tell a story from the road, to find them quoting my blog back to me... well at least it saved me having to talk too much.

And then I went home, put my feet up in front of the tv, and took it easy... right? ?.... errr nope... I went to a gig!

One of the many things that helped keep the pedals turning on crap days, was the thought that if I missed my flight home, I'd miss the Big Country gig. Whilst I was away, Big Country with Mike Peters had been on tour and Love Hope Strength Foundation had been swabbing people for the bone marrow donor list... and I had been missing it... big time! All the efforts of the volunteers had resulted in many people signed up on this tour, and the word of LHS spread to many more, and it was high time I got my arse in gear and did some work. So off to Southend we went. What a night! Loads of people signed up, met lots of new people, caught up with old friends and called up onstage by Mike Peters, the founder of the charity and all time legend. Luckily my weird suntan lines on my face hid my embarrassment but thank you Mike, I really appreciated it. The gig was brilliant, despite the fact that none of the band members felt well.. they all struggled through to give the audience a great night, certainly one I will never forget. My brother is now trained to swab and it was good to see Fitz, an outstandingly dedicated volunteer and to catch up with Mr Warden and the rest of the crew. It's great to be home...

Even the walk back to the car deserves a mention, purely for the Route 66 sign on top of one of the buildings... weird huh?

The drive home was pretty quiet, (fortunately Emma was driving as jet lag was starting to hit) as we were all knackered. We dropped Paul off and I was persuaded to go to A and E for my foot, which probably wasn't made better by jumping up and down at the gig but I cant help myself. To cut a long story short, after 2 and a half hours of waiting I was very restless and impatient and gave up, instead climbing the 6 flights of stairs (parker take note) to work for coffee, toast and a bit of a catch up at 4am!

I eventually got home and faced the task of unloading kit, unlocked my door.... and stopped dead in my tracks. My house was not only decorated with balloons and banners but had been cleaned from top to bottom, complete with new bedspread (apparently there were big discussions as to whether the teenage mutant ninja turtle one or the pink princess one was more 'suitable') and a Route 66 sign hanging on my wall. I was literally speechless... so thank you very very much to Emma and Jill for such a kind thought!

The homecoming was made complete out at dinner last night... I am so very lucky to have people like you guys to come home to... thank you xx

And so began the week... one which will be taking me to Ipswich, Nottingham, Doncaster and Grimsby, swabbing people with other fantastic volunteers for the bone marrow donor list. So if you have enjoyed my journey and are interested in GETTING ON THE LIST with LOVE HOPE STRENGTH FOUNDATION and DELETE BLOOOD CANCER, please go to www.deletebloodcancer.org.uk, where you can get a home swabbing kit, and www.lovehopestrength.co.uk for details of the charity and other events coming up. We always need volunteers to help with the swabbing, so if you would like to help other people save lives, drop me a message or go to The LHS website.

So to summarize the journey in a few words....tough, beautiful, emotional, raw and peaceful. Over 2400 miles (roughly) in 24 days of cycling - 2 hours later than scheduled arrival to friends with a gig to celebrate. Total so far raised now over £6000 - www.justgiving.com/Route66LHS.

Thank you once again to everyone for the support and to Mike Peters for Music and Inspiration
This is not the end... I will continue to dream of adventure and put those dreams into reality as life is short and can only be lived once... please keep an eye out on my blog and facebook page for ideas and plans of future adventures and LHS..
FIGHT BACK, DREAM ALOUD AND STAY ALIVE

Chapter 37 - In the search for the real life...

And that is nearly the end of this particular journey. I sit here nearly 2 weeks later, re-reading the blogs and adding some thoughts and it still doesn't seem real.

Possibly because I have yet to go back to work (going back tomorrow).

My first week back consisted of a few hundred miles in my car, going to Big Country gigs and swabbing people for the Bone Marrow Donor list whilst there. I absolutely love doing this as not only do I get to watch the legend that is Mike Peters on stage, I have made friends for life, who I caught up with, and meet new people all the time, whilst doing something that will hopefully benefit lots of people.

It did however result in lots of very late nights, which when combined with jet lag, isn't the best way to return to normal circadian rhythms. Which is possibly why, almost 2 weeks later, I am wide awake at nearly 2a.m. I did have a few days where I crashed on my sofa, catching up with the TV programmes that I missed.. (OMG Downton!!!) but after 3 days I'm now bored and looking for a way to fill the day, hence compiling this book!

Physically, I'm already concerned about my lack of exercise these past 2 weeks - jumping up and down at the gigs notwithstanding and am trying to curb my eating back to the level that it was at before my trip.

My foot continued to hurt and so I eventually went to see a G.P and got an X-Ray... results remain outstanding. The worst physical injury I appear to have received is the damage to the strength of my fingers. Initially both the 4th digits were unable to straighten or grip, a problem far more disturbing when I tried and failed to play my guitar! On a more serious note, I need my fingers to do my job and although my left hand has improved to the point of almost normal, my right hand continues to give me a bit of trouble. Hopefully it will improve with time as the other hand did and I will be left with no long lasting effects.

I continue to be touched by the generosity of family, friends and strangers who have donated to my bike ride. Donations are still trickling in but at the point of writing this, together we raised around £6450. A staggering amount considering I was initially aiming for £2000. I hope that I have also managed to spread the word of LHS to more people and maybe inspired some people to get out, conquer their fears and follow their dreams. If I have inspired just one person to do this, it will have been worthwhile.

Many people go on journeys in order to search for the 'real life'... I am lucky in that I finished my journey and came back to mine. I will remain indebted to everyone that supported me - I could not have done it without you.

If you are interested in finding out more about Love Hope Strength Foundation, please visit www.lovehopestrength.co.uk or www.lovehopestrength.org if in the USA.

To find out more about the Bone Marrow Donor list and how you can sign up online - please visit www.deletebloodcancer.org.uk for more information and a home swabbing kit.

If you want to keep up to date with any plans for further adventures from my point of view, I will be posting on http://route66LHSCycle.blogspot.com and my facebook page www.facebook.com/Route66LHSCycle

If you are interested in hearing the songs referred to throughout this blog, all appear on iTunes and many appear on Youtube or you can visit www.thealarm.com for more information about The Alarm and Mike Peters.

Lastly the music of Mike Peters has been integral to this ride. The songs that are referred to throughout the blogs are listed in Appendix 2.

They weaved the background to this ride and filled my days with inspiration.

Appendix 1 - Wildlife seen (dead or alive)
A complete list of the animals I came into contact with:

Owl (dead)
Condor (alive)
Condor (dead)
Snake (dead)
snake (alive)
Armadillo (dead)
Racoon (dead)
Skunk (dead)
Deer (dead)
Moose (alive) - at the Grand Canyon National Park
Tarantula (alive)
Prairie Dogs (alive and curious)
Groundhog (alive but shy)
Cat (dead)
Dogs (unfortunately alive and chasing me)
lizards (alive)
fox (dead) - just bones
frogs (alive)
roadrunner (alive and fast)
tortoise (dead)
vole (alive)
Stick insect (SID - alive)
Crickets (large ones)
locusts (alive

I was disappointed not to see another tarantula or a
rattlesnake!

Appendix 2 - Songs referred to in the blogs.

How the Mighty Fall
Last Ship Sails - Big Country
The Deceiver
True Life
The Message,
68 Guns
The Journey - Big Country
The Road
One Step closer to home
Absolute Reality
Broken Promised Land - Big Country
It's alright, It's ok
Down the Road
The Wind blows away my words
Rescue me
Breathe
My Town
Unsafe building
Fight back
No frontiers
Another Country - Big Country
Lead me through the darkness
Hardland
Trying to make it to the end of the world
Unbreak the promise
My Calling
Where were you hiding when the storm broke
Rocking in the free world
Strong - Big country
Life can be beautiful
Love Hope and Strength
Breaking Point

The Life you seek does not exist
Without a fight
Breed apart
In the Beauty of my surroundings
Search for the real life
Third Light

Thank you to Nicky Pritchard for this fantastic depiction of the ride!

Cover Art by Catherine Simpson - Thank you